A journal of nature & story

Get in touch

info@elementumjournal.com

Elementum Journal

PO Box 9205, Sherborne, Dorset
DT9 9DZ, United Kingdom

Connect

Twitter @elementumjrnl
Instagram @elementumjournal
Facebook @elementumjournal

Buy or subscribe online

www.elementumjournal.com/shop

Become a stockist

If you would like to stock
Elementum please contact us
info@elementumjournal.com

Cover & additional photography

by Owen Perry
Bella Coolla Estuary & Haida Gwaii
British Columbia, Canada

The Lost Words

Images from *The Lost Words* reprinted with
permission from Hamish Hamilton.

Images copyright Jackie Morris.
Word-spells copyright Robert Macfarlane.

Abandoned Mines

Surface and underground plan of the
Phoenix United Mines at Linkinhorne,
Cornwall. Thought to be drawn by
Henderson's surveyors c.1898. Reprinted
with permission Cornwall Records Office,
Reference MRO/3817/1.

Bing aerial view reprinted with
permission from Microsoft Corporation.

ISBN 978-0-9956740-1-1   ISSN 2398-6301
A CIP record for this book is available from the British Library.
Elementum is a biannual publication.

With grateful thanks to studio
assistant, Esme Armstrong

Printed in the UK
on FSC certified paper

ROOTS

EDITION THREE

To Murdo

With best wishes,

Jay

ELEMENTUM

CONTRIBUTORS

WRITERS & EDITORS

Jim Crumley

Tony Hoagland

Kathleen Jamie

Susannah Marriott

Kym Martindale

Robert Macfarlane

Wyl Menmuir

Catherine Mitchell

Martin Shaw

Colin Taylor

Alex Woodcock

Annie Worsley

PHOTOGRAPHERS & ARTISTS

Caroline Blythe

Rebecca Clark

Lucy Eldridge

Lucy Grant

Nicholas Hughes

Catherine Hyde

Jackie Morris

Owen Perry

Keith Russ

Leo Stockley

EDITORIAL & CREATIVE DIRECTION

Jay Armstrong

FOREWORD

Earlier this year I was fortunate to spend time with Scottish poet and writer Kathleen Jamie. She described writing poetry as 'a lengthy, conscious process that begins with acute observation.' This, as I am learning, is far from straightforward. It requires focus; it asks us to put aside expectations, pre-conceived ideas and prior knowledge, to make space for new perspectives. Piecing together this edition I am once again struck by the wealth of insight gained by our contributors from their 'acute observation', and from a desire to preserve the story of their findings for future generations.

This edition is about origins and things that lie hidden, about what we have lost and where to look to rediscover that knowledge. It is also about the interconnectedness of our fragile ecologies and the need to preserve species not only in their habitat but in language. We've travelled far afield and ventured deep underground, included voices from various nations, and explored a collaborative creative process that shaped a unique book. I'm thrilled to introduce to a wider audience the extraordinary lifetime's work of mining engineer Dr Keith Russ, who has singlehandedly digitally mapped hundreds of abandoned mines in Devon and Cornwall. Engineering science, art and social history intersect in his models and articulate in the most extraordinary way the human story of mining and our dependence on the earth's resources.

As for *Elementum*, much of the work we've put in recently has gone unseen, as roots often are. But I firmly believe that if we are to continue to pursue our vision of a print publication that maintains the highest possible content, production and ethical standards, then this season of quiet growing is as important as any other. Back in the spring, as I walked along a Pembrokeshire beach with artist Jackie Morris discussing these thoughts as well as old stories and new ideas, she said to me, 'We have to remember the children we once were – open and with all sorts of ideas in our heads.' I'll leave you with this and I hope, as you read this journal, that the contributions will spark your own childlike visions of other possibilities.

Jay Armstrong
Editor

CONTENTS

08   THE DARK BENEATH OUR FEET

UNEARTHLY TALES
FROM UNDERGROUND

Wyl Menmuir – Lucy Grant

18   THE WOLF TREE

AN AGELESS TREE,
AN ABSENT SPECIES

Jim Crumley – Catherine Hyde

28   DEIRDRE REMEMBERS
A SCOTTISH GLEN

MEDIEVAL IRISH POEM

Martin Shaw – Tony Hoagland – Rebecca Clark

32   ISLAND BEGINNINGS

REWILDING IN MAURITIUS

Colin Taylor – Lucy Eldridge

44   ILLUMINATING LOST WORDS

SPELLING ABSENCES
BACK INTO BEING

Jackie Morris – Robert Macfarlane – Jay Armstrong

64   LEAF TALK

CONVERSATIONS WITH
THE GREEN MAN

Alex Woodcock – Nicholas Hughes

76   ON RED HAIR AND BELONGING

ROUTES OF ANCESTRY
AND MIGRATION

Catherine Mitchell – Lucy Eldridge

86   AN HOUR TO SING

A JOURNEY OF FOLLOWING

Kym Martindale – Caroline Blythe

106   ABANDONED MINES

THE WORK OF ENGINEER,
KEITH RUSS

Keith Russ – Jay Armstrong

118   THE BONE CAVES

120   SECRETS OF LIMESTONE
AND WATER

THE CAVES OF INCHNADAMPH

Annie Worsley – Jackie Morris

124   THE REINDEER CAVE

DREAM OF THE BEAR

Kathleen Jamie – Jackie Morris

130   HAIDA GWAII

ISLANDS OF THE PEOPLE

Owen Perry

THE DARK
BENEATH OUR FEET

UNEARTHLY TALES FROM UNDERGROUND

Words: Wyl Menmuir
Illustration: Lucy Grant

Our relationship with caves is complex and deep-rooted. We cannot leave them alone, and the stories with which we fill them expose our need to explore the unknown and the suppressed, the subversive and the dangerous.

Wookey Hole, Death's Head Hole, Slaughter Stream Cave, Excalibur Pot. The names we give to the narrow cracks and caverns we find in the Earth's crust suggest fantasy landscapes rather than anything terrestrial. It's indicative of our deep-rooted collective fear of and fascination with the subterranean networks beneath our feet that we name them so transparently, in awe and terror, as mystical, unearthly domains.

It says something too about the potency of caves as symbols that we have imbued them with so many different meanings over time. For our forager ancestors, the daylight zone – the part of the cave into which natural light filters – offered protection and retreat from a dangerous world. Entrances to caves have been homes, places of pilgrimage, of sanctuary and refuge in times of war and disaster, spaces in which one could be enclosed by the Earth's solid arms.

Go a little further into the cave, into the twilight zone, the liminal space where the light starts to blend with darkness, and the meaning of the cave shifts. The literal starts to give way to the figurative and caves become spaces that are both sacred and profound. From the earliest times and in cultures across the globe, caves have been places of birth and rebirth, initiation and rites. Their walls have been the canvas for our earliest art – from the wild horses and mammoths of Lascaux in France to the ancient hand stencils found in Pettakere, Indonesia, and Cueva de las Manos (the Cave of Hands) in Patagonia. We sense the importance of these symbols, we feel a connection with our ancestors but time puts their original significance beyond our reach.

Go further still, into the dark zone where no natural light enters, and the meaning of caves shifts once more from the sacred to the mythical. The deep cave is often the entrance to the underworld, a vault that contains and suppresses our darker selves, keeping them out of sight and on the very edge of our consciousness. Digging into the rich seam of subterranean stories that runs back as far as the earliest known narratives – the *Epic of Gilgamesh* describes the hero Enkidu's voyage through buried passages to the underworld – it seems we have always been in equal part intrigued and appalled by the thought of the perpetually dark spaces beneath our feet. And rightly so. To delve deep into the cave is to willingly go beyond the reach of light, to confront the parts of ourselves we would rather stayed buried.

In Greek mythology, amid stories pitted with caves and underworlds, Tartarus, the subterranean prison of the Titans, was a terrifying chasm set aside for the gods' confinement, retribution and punishment. So strong was the image, it was retained by the Romans and subsequently made its way into Judeo-Christian mythology as the place where the rebel angels were imprisoned. Closer to home, Oweynagat – the cave of cats – in Rathcroghan (an archaeological site near Tulsk in County Roscommon, Ireland) was a hellsmouth, an entrance to the underworld. In Celtic mythology, Oweynagat is the threshold across which terrible creatures – ravenous cats, small red birds that withered living things, pigs that spread terrible decay, and the three-headed monster, Ellén Trechend – emerged to lay the land to waste at Samhain, the festival that marked the onset of winter. Norse mythology has its underworld too – the word cave in old-Norse is *hellir*, a term closely connected to that for the Norse realm of death, *hel*, from which we derive our word hell.   ⇥→

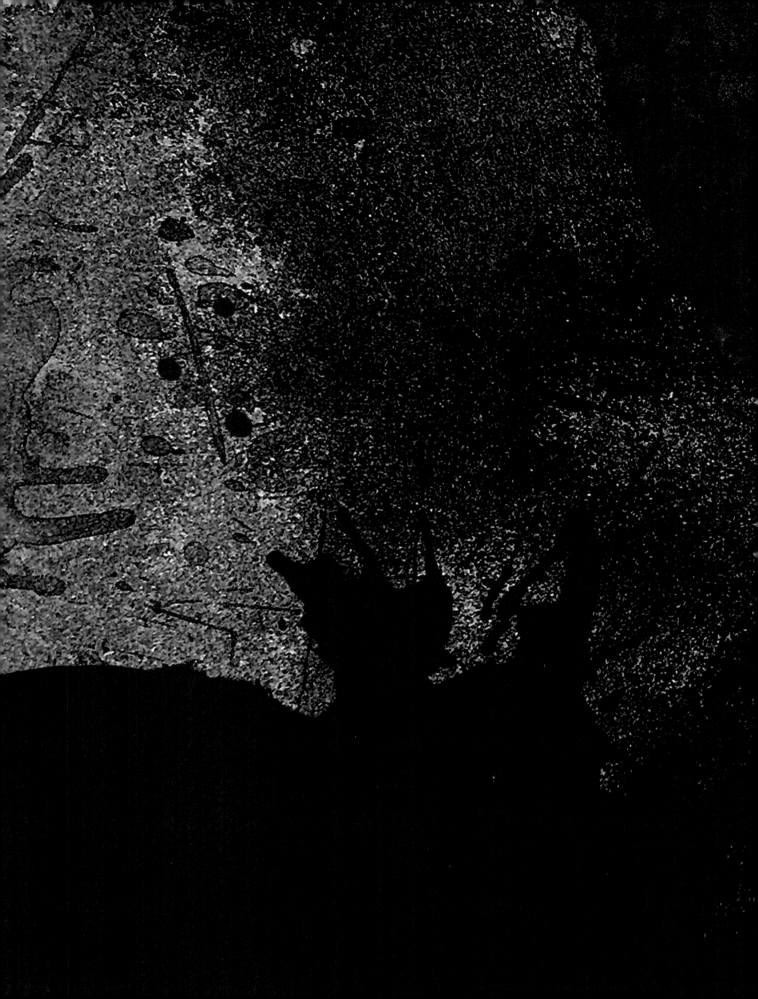

As a child, I was obsessed with the rumours that there was a maze of tunnels beneath the woods just outside the village in the foothills of the Pennines where I grew up. We were warned of the danger of these hidden tunnels in the woods, but this only served to entice us to search for them more thoroughly. My friends and I scoured the old chapel for signs of their entrances and spent days walking up and down the hillside searching for openings. Needless to say, we found none and we made do instead with caves that had been well explored before but still held a peculiar interest and were on our doorstep in the Peak District – Speedwell, Poole's and Treak Cliff caverns. They were places of wonder and transgression somehow and, while we knew many had been there before us, felt entirely otherworldly. Just a few steps in and as the darkness closed around we felt a hundred miles from the surface and from the familiar. The interest in these dark, wild places has stayed with me ever since, somewhere just beneath the surface. So when asked if I would like a tour of the caves at Cheddar Gorge as part of my research for a short story, I jump at it.

I arrive in the early morning before the cafés and shops have opened and walk down through the gorge. It is cool in the shade of the limestone cliffs and I watch a group of climbers as they attempt a route high overhead. Further down, at the entrance to Dreamhunters and Gough's Cave, the brightly coloured hoardings that advertise the caves jar with me. I have not visited the gorge before and my

expectation is at odds with the conspicuous markers of the tourist industry. I should not be so surprised. The caves at Cheddar have been popular with visitors since the 1830s, when one section was first opened by the commercially savvy George Cox who had tapped into the Victorian travellers' thirst for the awe-inspiring and sublime. Signs were erected shortly after, advertisements placed in newspapers, lighting installed, and footpaths created through the show caves that had been cleared and cleaned. I feel cheated. It feels sanitised, as though some of the layers of narrative have been stripped away by these conspicuous notices, by the infrastructure built up around them.

I am met by adventure writer and editor Patrick Kinsella and our guide, Paul Ballantyne. We don boiler suits, hardhats and head torches and bypass the queues at the turnstile. Paul leads us beyond the threshold past a plaster cast of Cheddar Man, the oldest complete human skeleton found in Britain (the original is now in London's Natural History Museum), and a little further on we pause to look at the stacks of cheese rounds that mature in the cave's constant temperature and humidity. Both are a little bemusing, as is the knowledge that over time these caves have been used as a gambling den and a mushroom farm.

Further in, at the cave's twilight zone, Paul stops to show us a rock carving of a mammoth discovered in 2007, believed to be about 13,000 years old. I stare at it long enough to make out the hind legs, the sweep of its back and a long tusk, though as I am squinting at it Paul says he's not convinced. It's so easy, he says, to see what you want to see, to impose a narrative onto lines in the rock. He suspects this mammoth has been willed into being by the strength of our desire to see it. The caves here flood so regularly, he says, he cannot see that any cave art would have survived that long. At this point there would have been little light, though now the show caves are so well lit that small forests of ferns grow beneath the lamps in niches in the wall.

Further in still, we turn off the well-trodden, well-lit main path, away from the families milling around and taking photographs. We make our way up over much less polished rock and the noise and partial light of the show caves fades behind us. Paul turns off the halogen side lamps in the cave and we duck into a passage, the roof of which slopes until we have to crawl, and we emerge into a large chamber. A few minutes in, I realise I am totally disorientated and yet we are just metres from the show caves. Paul introduces us to some of the cave's less explored passages and features. In a series of increasingly uncomfortable squeezes, I post myself on my back through 'the coffin', the roof millimetres from my nose, contort myself through a tunnel that, in shape, resembles a toilet U-bend, and then through a hole so tight I have to go through hands first to avoid becoming stuck. We climb on ladders over long drops, haul ourselves up through gaps in the rock and abseil from ledges into the darkness below.

In between the different caves, crawls and squeezes, Paul tells us stories about caving in more recent times. Stories about cavers trapped so deep in systems so remote that their remains have been left there, entombed where they died, or of traumatised survivors who returned to the surface carrying the bodies of their friends. These tales seem to echo, in some way, the archetypal stories of the dark zone, the deep cave as a place in which we confront our deepest fears.

We reach a smaller cave in which the roof tapers above to a thin crack and Paul tells us we can go no further. There is a small iron grate in the floor that leads down to a section of the cave that has not yet been explored. Some cavers suggest that this system connects to another, though no one has yet found a way through. The grate is tiny and the thought of going down through it into the confined depths we glimpse is truly terrifying. The image of Tartarus looms large.

On our way back through to the show caves, we stop for a while in the Boulder Cave, the chamber in which caver David Lafferty spent 130 days in total isolation in 1966. During this test of endurance Lafferty's sleep patterns changed completely, he lost all track of time and suffered hallucinations. It is a reminder that being underground is no more our natural environment than Everest's Death Zone. We switch our headlamps off and sit for a while in darkness so complete that it seems entirely alien. It is at this point I realise that we are not really, as we say, underground – we are in-ground. We are not below the rock but encased within it. The realisation of being so far out of my element brings on a strange and fleeting sense of panic, and I wonder whether Lafferty had similar thoughts in his four months here. The feeling passes and is replaced by another and altogether more enriching one. As I start to relax, the darkness and the silence become womblike, comforting and meditative. It is profoundly dark, so dark it's not possible for the eyes to adjust. I get a small sense of why we are so keen to fill these spaces with stories – once glimpsed, the dark voids cannot be unseen. We fill them with stories to explain them away, to make them more comprehensible. In reaching down into the physical depths, we may find dark reflections of our inner selves or discover something beautiful and profound. What we find in the cave is what we bring there – it is we who stare back at ourselves from the void. It occurs to me that possibly the complete darkness you can only find in-ground is vital to us, to balance the light with which we fill our lives. We need the dark wilderness, the reminder of the pre-human, beautiful and terrifying in equal measure.

After we leave, the strongest memory I take with me is that of the small grate in the furthest reaches of the cave. I want to leave it where it is, but it follows me to the surface and out into the light. Despite the hoardings and the adverts and the coaches in the valley, it's not hard to imagine that small hole, beyond the reach of the lights in the show caves, is an entrance to Tartarus, or that as from Oweynagat, a thousand ravenous red birds might fly, brought up from the deepest recesses of our minds. ✪

THE WOLF TREE

AN AGELESS TREE, AN ABSENT SPECIES

Words: Jim Crumley
Illustration: Catherine Hyde

Wolves are wiser than us when it comes to knowing what constitutes a healthy biodiversity. And their race-memory of this land and how to live in it is as long and as sound as the roots of our oldest tree, the yew. We would be wise to listen to them.

Wolves are not so long gone as you might think. Sometimes, here and there amid heartland tracts of Highland Scotland like the Black Wood of Rannoch or the Black Mount hills and woods around Loch Tulla, I have become aware of an absence and I put it down to wolves. That sounds finicky, I know, but such landscapes have a way of dislocating time. There is a harder-edged wildness at work there, and the sense of it reaches you almost like a scent, or the sound of it is in your ears like a threnody, for it laments its own incompleteness. For thousands of years – and until not so long ago as you might think – this was a land shaped almost as much by wolves as by ice, and the wolves were shaped by the forest. And now much of that forest is an absence too.

These are quiet places where a solitary traveller can still feel close to the land itself. In the far north of the world, and to this day, there is an awareness among the circumpolar tribes of the need to *listen* to the land. We have largely lost the skill but I think there was never a more important time to try and relearn it, to seek out those who still teach it. If we did, and if we took that skill out into old wolf heartlands like these, we would hear that the land is restless, that nature is ill-at-ease because what we like to call our 'stewardship' of the land has deprived nature of the essential tools it needs to perform at its utmost. I believe the absence of wolves is the most glaring manifestation of that ill-at-ease condition. If you listen to the land today, if you sit still and alone and silent in its midst, looking around you and cross-examining what you see and what you hear, the land might tell you that it still feels the absence of wolves, that it still mourns wolves, that the memory of them is immortal.

When Scots use the words 'immortal' and 'memory' in harness, we are usually referring to Robert Burns whom we celebrate every year with that cornerstone of the Burns supper address known as the Immortal Memory. He is as alive in our midst as he ever was. And it is quite possible that Robert Burns knew wolves. He would certainly have known wolf stories.

His parents, and especially his charismatic story-teller mother, Agnes Broun, were born into a Scotland already overflowing with wolf legends which included an obsession with 'last wolf' stories, even as the dwindling remnants of Scotland's wolf population scattered far and wide into the unpeopled corners of the land, there to make one last stand for nature.

The most preposterous of all our 'last wolf' legends (and that is really saying something) was, ironically, the last legend of all, and therefore the most durable. It claimed that the last of the race was killed in single-handed combat by a giant of a man called MacQueen up the strath of the River Findhorn in Morayshire, and in the year 1743. The story is, of course, fiction. It bears all the over-familiar hallmarks of a story-telling tradition which travelled west from the Holy Land with the spread of Christianity. Christ was the Good Shepherd, the people were his flock, the wolf was the enemy of the shepherd, and therefore the agent of the Devil. Almost always in last wolf stories, the hero is a giant (in MacQueen's case he was 6 feet 7 inches), a woman is walking alone or with her children across the hills in winter, usually at Christmas (the Christian origins of the tradition are never far away), she is attacked/half eaten/killed, and the heroic hunter sets out alone and slays the wolf, finally removing its scourge from the land.

The story became embedded so deeply in the human psyche that, incredibly, its message endures still – wolves attack and kill children and women (they rarely attack humans unprovoked, unlike some pet dogs). The Findhorn story was written down – but not until 1829 – by Sir Thomas Dick Lauder, a frustrated writer who was obsessed by Walter Scott, and used his invention to brighten up an otherwise mundane account of the traumatic Moray floods of that year. It is nothing more and

nothing less than a story, yet it has gone into the language and even into the literature of nature-conservation thinking as being the date when the wolf was finally obliterated. In that great endeavour, our ancestors chose to believe that they were successful. I don't think so.

There is no reason whatever to believe that human hands killed the last of our wolves. There is every reason to believe that, being wolves, the last of the race died old and alone, widely scattered and far from human gaze, their numbers having become too few to be sustainable. There is some reason to believe that a relict population lived well beyond 1743, perhaps even into the dawn of the nineteenth century.

Wolves came early to our post-ice-age land in the wake of the first recolonising trees, for woodland cover would consolidate a wide range of prey species. It is just possible that one tree in particular, and which is still living in Highland Perthshire, knows the full story – the arrival of the first explorer wolves, the golden age when they ruled the land on nature's behalf as overlords of biodiversity, and the long, slow decline to ultimate extinction in the face of relentless human persecution. The tree in question is the Fortingall Yew. It is impossible to estimate its age with any accuracy because yew trees die back from the centre of the trunk outwards. Very old yews are hollow, they have no annular rings, and this oldest yew of all is quite formless, a ragged copse of fragments. A clue to the majestic nature of its heyday is found in a discreet circle of short posts marking the girth of the trunk. It is sixty feet in diameter.

In 1998, TV botanist David Bellamy conducted his own investigation into the history of the Fortingall Yew and advanced the hypothesis that it could easily be 8,000–9,000 years old, and therefore the oldest living organism in the

world. It is certainly among Europe's oldest. More recent estimates have been more cautious, but it's all guesswork and whether it is 3,000 or 5,000 or 9,000 years old hardly matters. What does matter to me as a Scottish nature writer is its astonishing historical reach – it is an ambassador for all my land's post-glacial eras.

The so-called Great Wood of Caledon has been as mythologised as wolves, and was never the sun-snuffing, coast-to-coast shroud the Roman chroniclers and cartographers tried to make out. But whatever it may have amounted to in reality, it was at its greatest extent about 5,000 years ago. When you draw close to the Fortingall Yew, you are in the company of the only living eye-witness that can claim, 'I was there.' It is also the only reliable repository of thousands of years of *true* wolf stories. Take a wild guess, a really wild one, at how many wolves kept the company of such a tree, knew it for a landmark, relaxed in its cocoon of shadows. My guess is that you will underestimate twofold, fivefold, tenfold.

You can meet old Scots pines of three or four hundred years of age in the pinewoods of Rothiemurchus or Abernethy in Strathspey and feel confident these knew the brush of wolf fur. But no Scots pine living today can lay claim to even half of one millennium – the gap between the longest lived pines and the apparently limitless lifespan of the Fortingall Yew symbolises the very different nature of their relationship with wolves. These individual pines merely witnessed the wolves' decline and fall. The yew presided over the high-water mark of the native forest, the unchallengeable reign of the wolves, and the greatest diversity of species this land ever knew.

It is the simplest of nature's rules – an abundance of predators is only possible when there is a superabundance of prey. In the context of wolves, prey meant ungulates, the grazing tribes, primarily deer and wild cattle, so by definition the Great Wood (I think there were actually four great woods, widely separated) must have been an open forest with many grassland clearings and wetlands, all of which also meant perfect conditions for beavers. So the two great manipulators of northern hemisphere wilderness – wolf and beaver – were present in substantial numbers and widely distributed. They are also intrinsically connected, a fact underlined by the most intensively studied wolf reintroduction programme in history – at Yellowstone National Park in the northern United States.

When reintroduction began in 1995, there was only one small group of beavers in the national park. Once the wolves had begun to establish themselves, their presence changed the behaviour of huge numbers of elk so that these were constantly on the move and no longer browsed large areas of vegetation to the bone, and once regeneration began to flow from that benevolent process, the first animals from outside the national park to follow the wolves were beavers. Now they are restored to their former range throughout Yellowstone. The wolves's impact on the elk created the conditions for regeneration to resume, beavers moved in to exploit that regeneration creating wetlands and water meadows, which in turned created opportunities for water plants, insects, birds and a range of mammals up to and including moose. Meanwhile, wolf kills created a new source of food for everything from grizzly bears and golden eagles to pinewood ants and the things that pinewood ants prey on.

The Fortingall Yew is the still-living symbol of all that. It invites you to consider the possibility of immortality. Science has never been enough to explain away the longevity of yew trees, but the yew is well rooted in the imagination and the imagery of human history. In Scotland, the further west you go, and the further back for that matter, the more tenacious and more potent the imagery.

John Knox liked to preach under yew trees, which may or may not have been a nod to an ancient Celtic tradition already old when Christianity was born, and which associated yew trees with sacred sites. It is also possible that an old yew tree's canopy of gloom was the perfect fit for the darker shades of his theology. The Royal Company of Archers, founded in seventeenth-century Scotland, is employed today as a ceremonial bodyguard of the monarch on away-days to Scotland and still carries yew longbows. English archers used yew longbows to particularly telling effect in the landmark encounters of our mutual history, not least at Flodden, a battle from which only the efficiency, strength and pliability of yew wood emerged with any credit.

That last great flourish of the yew bow as a battlefield weapon was a kind of epitaph for a tradition that was shown to be much older than many of us had imagined with the discovery in 1991 of the Ice Man in a frozen glacier in the Alps on the border of Italy and Austria. His astoundingly well-preserved Stone Age body was accompanied by an axe handle and a bow stave, both made of yew. Apart from anything else, there was never a more telling demonstration of yew wood's capacity to resist rot and damp, which may also explain why it was the wood of choice for many bagpipe makers. An instrument that had to spend its working life in Highland Scotland and live in black-houses would surely have need of such qualities. One way or another, and for thousands of years, the roots of our story and the yew's story have been irrevocably intertwined. In the twenty-first century, a quiet hour in the company of the Fortingall Yew suggests – to this nature writer at least – that we still have things to say to each other.

As a species, we have always valued roots. They are the source of our own story. Digging down among them, the tap root and the myriad offshoots, we like to unearth the evidence of the coalescing generations which made our lives possible. Most of us can gather in a couple of centuries before the trail goes cold. But the tap root of us all, and all our fellow travellers, is the land. The land is our common ancestor. We can follow its story ten thousand years back to the last Iron Age, and then – at least for those of us who are not geologists – the trail goes cold. The land as we recognise it today began when the ice backed off. Then the trees came. Then those other shapers of the land, wolf and beaver, followed. Then our hunter-gatherer selves.

And now, in twenty-first century Scotland, the beaver is back among us. Restored as an officially recognised native species in November 2016, it begins to nourish its own roots (thanks to its race memory of the ages) in the very landscapes in which it once thrived. As the species expands east from its official trial area in Argyll and west from its unofficial reintroduction on Tayside (from wildlife park escapees and the activities of what you might call nature conservation's provisional wing), what ancient wisdoms are exchanged as beavers edge past Fortingall and catch the scent of its singular yew tree? What kind of precedent have we established with this remarkably enlightened reintroduction? They enrich us, yew tree and beaver, because they deal in the simplest of nature's eternal truths. How long, do you suppose, before they – and we – thrill once more to what the American writer Catherine Feher-Elston calls 'wolfsong'?

A few years ago, I made two radio programmes for BBC Radio 4 about the relationship between wolves and people. They were titled *The Real Wolf* as a counterweight to the tonnage of unreal wolf propaganda which still litters and obscures the path to a more thoughtful relationship, and to reintroduction. In Norway, I interviewed two wildlife film-makers who had spent eight years making a television documentary about a single pack of Norwegian wolves. Towards the end of our time together I asked them what the sound of wolves howling meant to them. The less confident of the two, and with the less fluent English, suddenly found his tongue, and in halting phrases, which somehow empowered his words, he said this:

'You sit there in the winter times. Hoping that something will happen. You freeze a little. You take a little cup of tea. And you're looking. And looking. At trees full of snow. Nothing happens. Maybe you hear a little bird.

'And then you hear this noise. Starting very low, and you're thinking, 'Where is it? Where is it?' You know? You can feel how your whole body is looking for where the wolf is. And this voice, you bring it with you, in the body, for many, many, many days.'

Ever since that day, I have learned to feel the absence of the wolf in my own land, the absence of its voice, my whole body is looking for where the wolf is. And sometimes, sitting alone and listening, I hear the land cry out to its brother. ☸

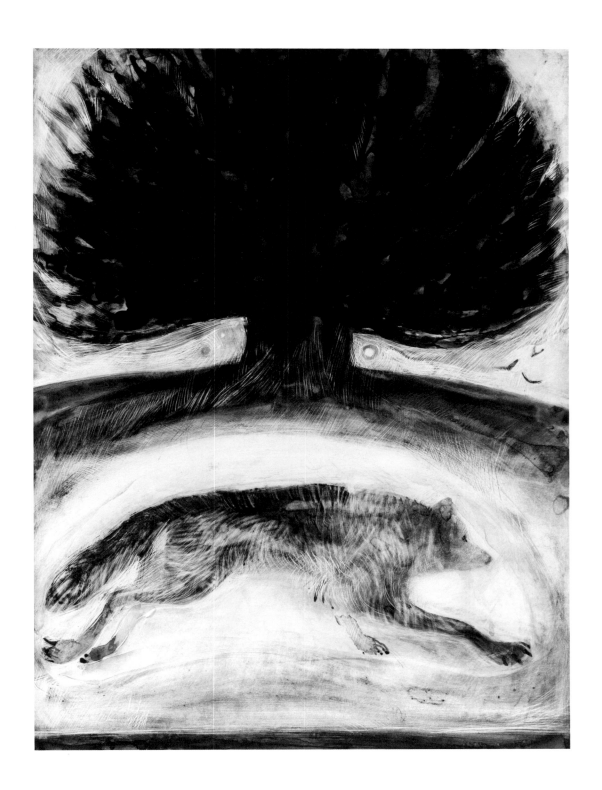

DEIRDRE REMEMBERS A SCOTTISH GLEN

MEDIEVAL IRISH POEM
Author Unknown

Illustrator: Rebecca Clark
Translated: Martin Shaw & Tony Hoagland

Glen of my body's feeding:
crested breast of loveliest wheat,
glen of the thrusting long-horned cattle,
firm among the trysting bees.

Wild with cuckoo, thrush, and blackbird,
and the frisky hind below the oak thick ridge.
Green roof that covered a thousand foxes,
glen of wild garlic and watercress,
and scarlet-berried rowan.

And badgers, delirious with sleep, heaped fat in dens
next to their burrowed young.
Glen sentried with blue-eyed hawks,
greenwood laced with sloe, apple, blackberry,
tight-crammed between the ridge and pointed peaks.

My glen of the star-tangled yews,
where hares would lope in the easy dew.
To remember is a ringing pain of brightness.

ISLAND BEGINNINGS

REWILDING IN MAURITIUS

Words: Colin Taylor
Illustration: Lucy Eldridge

When endemic plants and animals vanish from islands they are lost forever. From his tree-top office in the Indian Ocean, the man who helped conserve the rarest bird in the world remembers what roots him in the fragile ecologies of islands.

Perched 40 metres up on a swaying wooden platform within touching distance of the topmost fronds of a Japanese Cedar, I stare out at dawn over the canopy. My view is of the steep uninterrupted rainforest slopes of a long-extinct volcano. Far below, at the foot of the mountain, I can see the alluvial coastal plain with its expansive fields of sugarcane. Beyond that, the coast, fringed half a mile out with white surf at the coral edge, like the island is place-set on a delicate lace doily. Thereafter, the vast tablecloth of the deep blue Indian Ocean and on to the Southern Ocean and Antarctica thousands of uninterrupted miles away. But for the fact that humans have cut down the lowland forest for sugarcane to sweeten European palates, it's an easy journey of the imagination to believe I could be the only human alive enjoying the early morning sunshine on the island paradise that is Mauritius.

Far below me is a still, dank, humid world of moss-covered boulders, streams and dripping tree ferns. I find myself in this precariously beautiful location fulfilling the terms of my 'just work it out as you go along' job description. I'm looking out for the early-morning courting of the pink pigeon (*Nesoenas mayeri*), a large, engagingly tame, pink-bodied, chestnut-tailed bird. It's September 1989 and I know little about this bird other than there are maybe just nineteen of them left in the wild and a further few breeding pairs held in a handful of zoos around the world.

A few weeks previously I had arrived on the island with only a rucksack full of clothes, a notebook, a pencil and a return ticket to an uncertain future with no plan. I was part of a small team of survey biologists on a six-week expedition to record ecological findings on Round Island, an uninhabited, sun-baked ash dome volcano island to the north of Mauritius. At the end of this worthy work my colleagues had jobs, commitments or relationships to take them back to Britain. I did not.

I met a man called Carl. He asked me to work for him in the forests. He showed me a picture of a large colourful bird and told me it was a pink pigeon that only existed in the wild on Mauritius. He asked me to count as many as I could find and locate their nests. As inducement, he offered a motorbike so I could get from the coast to the forest and said if I did well then Gerry, a friend of his, would pay a small bursary for my keep. I accepted and became the man who worked with the rarest bird in the world from an office in the tree-tops.

The pink pigeon is rare. As a squab it's vulnerable to predation in the nest from hitch-hikers that arrived 400 years ago with the first humans to set foot here. Stowaway rats scurried ashore and the ship's cats chased after them. Crab-eating macaques leaped from sailors' shoulders for better pickings on land. They all found life infinitely more tolerable on an island with no natural predators. The local wildlife had not evolved to fear other species so became easy prey. Indian mongoose were brought in to clear up the plagues of rats the cats had ignored in favour of the endemic wildlife, but the mongoose too soon forgot about the rats.

From my arboreal vantage point I picture these newcomers spreading rapidly across the island like a drop of oil on still water, outcompeting the native fauna and fauna, chomping through these fragile ecosystems. When plants and animals vanish from islands they are lost forever. Our hand in this loss is legend. An early casualty was the dodo (*Raphus cucullatus*). A descendant of the humble pigeon with no natural predators, it had no need for flight and evolved to root around the leaf litter of the ebony forests doing what big pigeons do, eating. This was until it became the visiting sailors's meal and sport of choice. The last one was sighted in 1662, less than 65 years after its first discovery.

I like living, working and wandering in the same sub-tropical forests as the dodo. I keep alive the romantic notion of finding a forgotten forest corner, inaccessible valley or mountain plateau where a remnant population survives. I dream of being the first person to set eyes on the bird since a Dutch sailor raised his musket to the last one 350 years ago. From up here in the canopy it's clear that their extinction has not been the only loss. The passing of the dodo has meant that another species is waning – the grandest tree in the forest, the tambalacocque (*Sideroxylon grandiflorum*), is few and far between. It's believed the species evolved with the dodo. Its gizzard contained stones that were thought to soften the hard nut shell which the large lumbering bird would later deposit in the leaf litter, the seed germinating in its own rich compost heap – a welcome boost for any tree, accelerating its growth up into the sunlight many metres above. No dodo, no germinating tambalacocque. Fewer trees, less fruit for the endemic echo parakeet (*Psittacula eques*) – and so it goes on. Take out one species and the interconnectedness of the ecosystem reshapes, threatening the extinction of others. My benefactor, Gerry, puts it well, 'The world is as delicate and as complicated as a spider's web. If you touch one thread you send shudders running through all the other threads. We are not just touching the web, we are tearing great holes in it.' He's fairly adept with words is Gerry. Carl tells us that if we do nothing then all we will be left with is cockroaches, rats and feral pigeons. He's talking about a wider world than our little Indian Ocean island. We must focus our conservation efforts on species other than pandas, rhinos and orangutans; the lesser known species we're working with here are our early warning signals for the harm that come with loss of diversity.

Any conservation job means accepting unsocial hours and anti-social working conditions. When I set out from my damp canvas ridge tent before dawn this morning it was in the company of the night's tropical rain, which soaked me to the bone. We enjoy about seven meters of rain per year; about ten centimetres a day in the wet season, and it's a muddy commute to the part of the forest I call my office. Now, after a few hours up top in the heat of the southern Indian Ocean, the heavy khaki cotton shirt and combat trousers I'm wearing have dried to me. The mosquitoes and deer fly that swarm below the canopy can march right through lighter cotton, so the thick canvas clothes I've had made protect me from their piercing attention. In these sweltering, damp hours while I'm waiting for the fleeting glimpse of a large pink and chestnut-brown pigeon I have plenty of time to think. To dream if you will.

And there you have it. Islands to me are places to dream. A place that even in its name raises a question about itself. Is land? I love them. Not all islands, just those large enough that we can eke out an existence but not so large they cannot be traversed in a day or so. Places with their own weather, water, tides and terrain that produce a unique culture and set of rules for surviving that piece of sea-locked land. A place with a coastline and wrapped with a simple horizon that is difficult to reach. A place with obvious boundaries, finite resources, and a lack of choice that forces me to figure out the 'how'. How am I going to survive here? How am I going to communicate with the outside world? How am I going to thrive? How am I going to find me? Sitting up in my tree this idea animates me – and over the years that follow I will seek out and live on many islands in a variety of guises, be it as biologist, nature warden or police officer. I feel me on an island.

My fanciful dreams of dodos remind me of Charles Darwin on another island. In 1831 the Victorian naturalist set off on a five-year voyage around the world to the island location of his famed eureka moment, the Galápagos. Whiling away hours up here in the canopy, I imagine Captain Robert FitzRoy setting him ashore and Darwin directing his assistant or 'fiddler and boy to poop cabin', Syms Covington, to bag a brace or two of finch species. There he is, back aboard HMS Beagle on the long haul across the Pacific to Tahiti, sitting in his cabin cogitating over his embalmed avifauna. Pondering the significance of bill shapes and plumage, he pens notes with a niggling hunch, a hunch that later became a theory and the foundation for *On the Origin of Species*.

On its journey across the Indian Ocean, The Beagle harboured up for ten days here on 'Île Maurice'. Darwin climbed a mountain, Le Pouce, and wandered lonely through the cloud forests carpeting the slopes of extinct volcanoes. He rode an elephant – a curio imported for the pleasure of gentry – and went to the opera. Like me, he was taken to muse 'How pleasant it would be to pass one's life in such quiet abodes'. Not if you had been a dodo. The trick Darwin missed was not to recognise that the wonder of cataloguing the plethora of species amounts to little if they are left as pinned specimens in dusty drawers or intricately drawn plates in worthy tomes. He sailed home, seemingly without a thought for highlighting to humanity the fragility of island ecologies, where even in the nineteenth century endemic flora and fauna were quickly vanishing forever due to human mismanagement.

In 1979, 148 years after Darwin set out, a gangly Welshman with an equally questioning mind pitched up on these island shores. A resourceful biologist, Carl Jones had been employed by a conservation organisation to travel to Mauritius and close down a failing project. A task, he gleefully says, he spectacularly failed to achieve. When he first arrived Carl found just four Mauritius kestrels (*Falco punctatus*) left on the island. A single female incubating a clutch of eggs halfway up one of these volcanoes was all that sat between a species and its extinction. The rarest bird in

the world, its numbers had been depleted by habitat destruction and indiscriminate DDT use in the 1960s and 70s. This kestrel had evolved on an island with no land mammals other than huge squabbling fruit bats and had adapted long legs to extend its reach when hunting geckos in the dense ebony forests. But the apex predator for an island 30 by 40 miles and 800 miles from the nearest continent was on its last metatarsals. I image Darwin pointing at the bird on the nest, Covington shooting, then stuffing it and blowing the eggs. Not Carl. He rolled down his sleeves to protect himself from these interminable mosquitoes and in the Mauritian rainforests applied the skills gained in his youth raising kestrels in the hills of Carmarthenshire. He took an idea from the valleys – supplementary feeding in the wild and a ruse called double-clutching – and increased the Mauritius kestrels' rate of breeding. He couldn't do it all on his own and over decades took on a succession of eager 'fiddlers and boys (and girls) to poop cabin', or as we were known in the twentieth century, 'volunteers'.

By the time I join Carl, still in the early years of his brilliant career, he has increased the number of Mauritius kestrels to over 50 and is adapting his techniques to save two other endangered comrades of the dodo – the pink pigeon and echo parakeet. In the late 1980s these are jointly the rarest birds in the world, with a total population of under 40 of each species.

And so we work on multiple fronts, trapping feral cats and mongoose, baiting rats and scaring off the monkeys. My part in the double-clutching is sitting here at the top of the tallest tree in this remote rainforest every humid morning for months on end looking out over the canopy and listening for the mating call of a pink pigeon. The trick is to spot where in this dense dark-green canopy the pink bird is nesting, then shimmy up that tree with a rotten wooden ladder and take the first eggs from the nest to hatch under a host species, Barbary doves (*Streptopelia roseogrise*a), in an aviary many miles away. The pigeons abandon that nest in a despondent huff, but a couple of weeks later grunt at each other in courting ritual, shrug and build another. This second clutch we also take but replace with plastic eggs so the parents stay happy and sit in incubation. Monkeys and rats soon discover that there's nothing tasty about a hard plastic egg. When their clutch of eggs hatches in the safety of our aviaries we return one squab to the parents none the wiser. It's funny to see a pigeon sitting on a plastic egg one moment and the next finding a large three or four-day-old squab in the nest. In this way, from one pair of birds we rear three or four birds a season. Without our intervention, and while hostilities continue between pigeon and alien predators, their breeding rate is disastrously low.

There were 20 pink pigeons in the wild when I arrived. Three years later when I left the island there were about 40; now there are some 400, and 400 parrots where there were less than 20.

There are now verdant islands where there were bare degraded volcanoes, giant tortoise have been reintroduced to graze on native vegetation, and flocks of olive white-eyes and Mauritius fodies, Gunther's geckos and keel-scaled boas are all doing their thing in greater numbers.

I have lived on many islands since Mauritius. I am drawn to, fascinated by, their natural state; I gain a sense of worth from helping to fill in the heavy footprints that destructive human intervention has left. I'm not a traditionalist but it's important to me that if something existed on an island it should continue to do so for as long as nature intended. There's the counter-argument that as mankind is also part of nature, then extinction at our hands is as much a part of that cosmic plan as anything else. If that is the case, then it is also true that we can be part of the solution and reverse the ill effects.

While I perched on a branch like a great ape, having found the perfect location to philosophise and ponder islands, Carl remained grounded, going on to become Professor Carl Jones who has averted the extinction of more species of animals than any other known individual. In 2016 he was awarded the greatest honour in conservation, the Indianapolis Prize. Gerry, I soon learned, was the philanthropic Gerald Durrell OBE, who among other things set up the Durrell Institute of Conservation and Ecology and wrote such timeless classics as *My Family and Other Animals* and *Golden Bats and Pink Pigeons*. Through his zoo in Jersey (now the Durrell Wildlife Park), he funded the pink pigeon project and reared the captive birds we sent back. From the island home of the creature that epitomises extinction, they nurtured a generation of conservation biologists working in every corner of the world to restore balance to our fragile ecology and help repopulate the ark. ☽

ILLUMINATING LOST WORDS

SPELLING ABSENCES BACK INTO BEING

With drawings by Jackie Morris and word-spells by Robert Macfarlane
Interview & Photography: Jay Armstrong

We spent time with artist and author Jackie Morris shortly after she had finished work on a unique project – a collaboration with author Robert Macfarlane to produce a book for all ages that seeks to conjure back into the language and the landscape words that were becoming lost to children. Simple words like 'acorn', 'conker' and 'starling'. They chose twenty 'lost' words and created for each a triptych of paintings – the first captures the absence of the plant or creature within its habitat; the second is a gold icon expressing its essence; in the third, it returns into its landscape. Robert's word-spells, accompanying the icon and intended to be read aloud, summons the image and word back into being.

The reason for this book? A recent research paper by conservationists at Cambridge University found that children between the ages of eight and eleven were significantly better at identifying common Pokémon characters than common species of British wildlife. Another survey showed that three-quarters of British children spend less time outdoors than prisoners. While children's knowledge and experience of nature is being lost, we're also undergoing a drastic reduction of species and habitat. More than half of species in the UK are in decline, and most of us are unaware of this loss.

Against this backdrop, we talked with Jackie about old words and new stories, the importance of observing the natural world and seeing with sharper focus. We bring together the working notebooks of both writer and illustrator, and gain unique insight into how the roots of this project took hold, and how shape emerged from openly responding to another artist's process and, above all, mutual respect and wonder for the living world. The resulting book is beautiful, sometimes eerie and perhaps, most of all, magical.

When I heard that words like 'bluebell' and 'heron' and 'acorn' were being lost to children, even 'kingfisher' – that one cut me most – I wanted to find a way of expressing how important this loss was. If a word exists then it tells a child it has value, that it is important.

As a child, you can be so open. Children see the world differently – it's as if they have a sharper focus. I think you lose this as you get older, once there are so many other things crowding your mind. When I was a child, I sensed that the earth was one living organism and that it all worked together – and now I'm an adult I've found out that there is a theory for this, a name, the Gaia principle.

I grew up in a town longing for the countryside. My dad would take me for walks and show me different wild flowers; we would watch where skylarks tumbled down so we could find their nests. He was a great storyteller and he told me the stories of the animals and plants; he showed me how to look and I learned the names from him. It's made me realise that it only takes one generation not passing on this knowledge and it's lost.

I thought of making a book, a wild dictionary, with a gold-leaf icon of each lost animal or plant and the word's definition beside it. I chose gold leaf because you get a luminosity, a soul; it's not just a simple representation. I asked Robert Macfarlane if he'd write a foreword for the book, but he saw something else there. His first idea was for a novel, but we felt the need not only to show the absence of the words but to spell them back into both language and landscape – an incantation and a spelling-out.

At that point we had no shape, and then Robert stated writing acrostics – beautiful pared-down prose. This brought to the images a sense of poetry, of wonder. One of the first pieces he wrote is 'Otter', and it starts –

Otter enters river without falter – what a
supple slider out of holt and into water …

You can just feel the animal moving. And here's 'Wren' –

When wren whirrs from stone to furze the world around
her slows, for wren is quick, so quick she blurs the air
through which she flows …

I mentioned to Rob the importance of keeping your own voice when writing for children; don't change it. Children step up to you, you don't need to step down to them. We have to remember the children we once were – open, and with all sorts of ideas in our heads. The language in this book has not been compromised and Rob's writing is different to the prose people know him for – it's poetry. But he doesn't call them poems – he calls them spells.

First, I painted a perfectly good raven thinking what could Rob possibly write that would make me do it any differently. But then he wrote 'Raven' and that was it, I had to repaint it – I suppose that's the difference between decorating a book with nice drawings and illustrating it, illuminating the words with other meanings.

Rock rasps, what are you?
I am Raven! Of the blue-black jacket and the
boxer's swagger, stronger and older than peak
and boulder, raps Raven in reply.

Air ask, what are you?
I am Raven! Prince of Play, King of Guile,
grin-on-face base-jumper, twice as agile as
the wind, thrice as fast as any gale, rasps
Raven in reply.

Vixen ventures, what are you?
I am Raven! Solver of problems, picker of
locks, who can often outsmart stoat and
always out-think fox, scoffs Raven in reply.

Earth enquires, what are you?
I am Raven! I have followed men from forest
edge to city scarp: black shadow, dark
familiar, hexes Raven in reply.

Nothing knows what you are.
Not true! For I am Raven, who nothing cannot
know. I steal eggs the better to grow, I eat
eyes the better to see, I pluck wings the
better to fly, riddles Raven in reply.

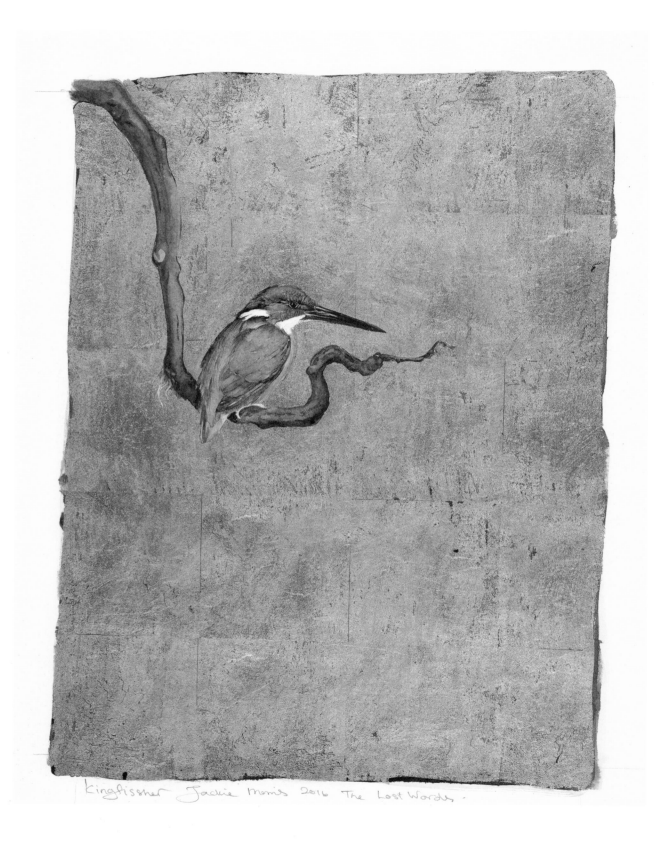

Kingfissher Jackie Morris 2016 The Lost Words.

I was very lucky to be able to find most of the twenty words we were spelling back in the garden or nearby. There are ferns growing up my house and I saw a weasel running in and out of the stone wall. The magpies built their nest just outside my window, and when I was walking on the hill behind my house, I almost trod on an adder. It was the most golden snake I'd ever seen – and that's the adder in the book. I've also spent a lot of time lying down in long grass looking at dandelions – looking and observing is my research.

A lot of things happened around the drawings – perhaps I was noticing more, I don't know, but wrens haunted my days when I was painting 'Wren'. Every time I went out for a walk it seemed they were following me. I'd come back from the beach with the dogs to a wren underneath my van in the car park. It was all very strange.

Rob had similar experiences – when he was walking at Orford Ness in Suffolk, an incredible, almost apocalyptical industrial landscape of deserted military buildings on a spit of land, he looked up and there, above this dark ditch, was a kingfisher sitting 'on the snag of a stick'. And this is what he wrote. Every book starts with questions, and both of us somehow found the answers we needed.

Finding the absences – and painting an absence in a landscape – was the hardest part for me. But those were the pages that became most interesting – they have a kind of visual poetry, and thinking through the ideas of absences in nature made the book fascinating for me.

'Heron' was the first piece I tried – the icon was easy enough, then I painted a heron in a landscape and another landscape without. It wasn't working, and I thought I couldn't do it. This can happen with books – you have a good idea, you're all fired up, and then you can't do it.

I spent time with my friend, zoologist and children's writer, Nicola Davies, who asked, 'Can't you pare it back and do something a bit more abstract?'

I walked up the hill behind my house with my new puppy, Pi, her first walk off the lead, and she brought me back a raven's feather – a gift that became 'Absence of Raven'. For 'Absence of Otter' I considered footprints, but they aren't really an absence. I ended up with just the bubbles on an empty page.

Robert wrote the foreword and I wanted to paint a picture of him that sums up his spirit and his soul – it's obvious to me that he's a lean running mountain hare.

As for me? It's got to be the heron. I'm forged from a long line of ironworkers in the Black Country – my gran was a nail and chain maker and my uncle from the age of four worked the bellows in the foundry. A hardy lot.

Here hunts heron. Here haunts heron.
Huge-hinged heron. Grey-winged weapon.

Eked from iron and wreaked from blue and
Beaked with steel: heron, statue, seeks eel.

It's been the most intense period of work – drawing what's not there, and with a sense of purpose, and trying to keep the magic, the poetry in it.

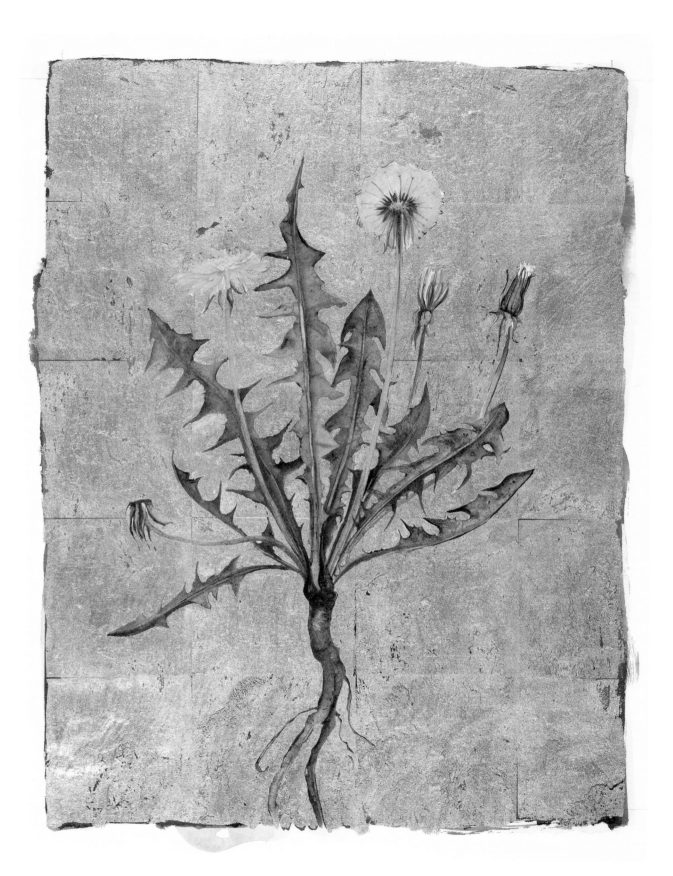

The naming of things, knowing the names of things, and seeing things more fully – this is what making this book has taught me to do. I thought I was quite aware, but it's taught me to look more closely, to see things differently.

Dandelions will never be the same now. When I painted them, I saw them in all their different parts – from when there's a flower bud to when it opens, the tiny stamens inside, the leaves in circles like the hands of a clock, and their colour which is beyond saffron, where red meets gold. And then as it folds, some kind of magic happens – almost like a caterpillar and chrysalis – and the flower turns into flight-ready seeds. It can happen every day in front of us and yet we take it for granted. When I was a child I would stop and watch the dandelion seeds blow in the wind – I want to do more of that again now.

When I was painting 'Bramble', I saw for the first time that if you look at the underside of the leaves, even when they are red in autumn, they are silver beneath. And 'Heather' – I'd always seen it as a purple wash, but look closely and you'll see that each flower is a tiny bell. Now, when I drive past hedges, I don't just see the green, I see ferns, nettles and celandine.

Do we need bluebells? I do. I need tigers, too. I may never see a tiger in the wild, but it doesn't matter because it's not about me. And I think that's what I wish more people would realise – it's not about us, it's not about humans – this is an ecosystem and everything is linked. If we take out one piece, and one piece more, and then another piece, eventually it all collapses.

If I look out the window now, there's no kingfisher, no otter, no heron. But just because we can't see them doesn't mean they're not there. They're very present, but they've become absent from our conversations, from our consciousness, from our children's language. Rob and I hope this book will help ensure that they don't disappear any further. I want the book to open up people's hearts and eyes to what's there; so that people notice, are in that moment, see what we have. Instead of looking at films of lions, to get out and find the sparrows. This is not a children's book, it's just a book, and I hope one that will give readers dreams – of wild ravens and diving kingfishers. ✲

A Richness of wrens Jackie Morris 2016 The Lost Words by Robert Macfarlane

AFTERWORD

THE GOLDFINCH SPELL

The goldfinch spell was written after we'd finished *The Lost Words*. By that time the goldfinch - those bright little birds that gather in 'charms' in our landscape – had become for both of us the book's totem creature, and also a sign of hope, for goldfinch populations are rocketing in Britain, unlike many of the other species in the book.

I wrote the spell one afternoon, when the news from America and indeed from around the world was pitch-dark. And I wrote it sitting by the bed of my grandmother, who is 101 years old, and who I'd travelled that day to be with. She was asleep when I arrived, so I sat by her bed, holding her hand every now and then, feeling strangely peaceful in her presence, thinking of the century she had seen, from the First World War into which she was born, all the way through to Trump's presidency. It was an odd kind of human deep time to dwell in for a while, and I wrote the goldfinch spell resting my notebook on my knee, thinking about the good in the world, and the ill it holds too; about our need for hope, even in the darkest of times.

Later, my grandmother woke up, and we watched Antiques Roadshow for a while together, and held hands again.

– Robert Macfarlane

God knows the world needs all   the good it can get right now — and

Out in the gardens, the woods,   goldfinches are gilding the land for free,

Leaving little gifts of light :   a gleam for the teasel, a glint for the tree.

Didn't you hear their high   scattered song, their bright twitter,

falling around you as flecks,   as grains, as glitter?

imagine the loss of their   lustre, the lack of their sheen;

no more shimmer, an unsettling absence of gilt.

charm on, goldfinch,   charm on — and

heaven help us when   all your gold is gone.

Jackie Morris
2017

Robert Macfarlane
2017

LEAF TALK

CONVERSATIONS WITH THE GREEN MAN

Words: Alex Woodcock
Photography: Nicholas Hughes

Place there is none.
We go backwards and forwards and there is no place.

St Augustine, *Confessions*

The Green Man can be found carved on Gothic churches across Europe. It has a complicated and often elusive history, and its shadowy presence invites us to connect with aspects of life we find similarly obscure or difficult to access.

The first record I bought was by Duran Duran. It was a seven-inch single, the year 1983. I was ten. I'd stopped seeing ghosts; now I had pop. It was enough and not enough. I place the candle on the metal stand and drop a fifty pence piece into the box. The column behind these tiny flames is made from a pale limestone, probably Caen, the church is St Thomas the Martyr, Winchelsea, in East Sussex. A Thursday. I'm thinking of a friend, recently deceased. I'm thinking of the second-hand books by the door. In my peripheral vision I can see the Green Man carved on the fourteenth-century tomb to my left, the reason for my visit today. I stand still and watch my candle burn, a single point of light among many others. I am glad of the silence.

Then I moved on. Depeche Mode was the next one; the third I can't remember. My friend Nick, or Nik as he preferred by then, introduced me to metal, Matt to the Sisters of Mercy. By the end of the eighties I was a fully-fledged goth, trawling charity shops for long coats and buying tight black jeans from Brighton, the nearest place I could get them back then. I grew my hair long and studied medieval history, feeling closer to the past than the present. But really, the connection I felt with this eerie music had crept in early. I'd seen Bauhaus on Top of the Pops when I was nine, a terrifying performance of white light and black hair and jagged guitars. I was mesmerised. Watching it again recently online it seems almost comical, the most threadbare theatre, as pompous and ridiculous as any other goth band that I grew to love; but its power remains undiminished. The song was a cover, and in their hands Bowie's once futuristic Ziggy Stardust seemed like a relic, something dug up out of the ground, with Bauhaus themselves the starry-eyed archaeologists. On national TV there'd been a sort of slip in time; somehow I knew even then that part of me felt comfortable there, perhaps even belonged in that gap.

I sit down on a nearby pew. Time seems to have different speeds in different places. It feels slow here, pooling around the tombs and the flames. This morning, as I was brushing my teeth and my eighty-three year old Dad was listening to the radio, I'd thought about coming over to the church. In my mind I could see masonry, dark like an engraving, the month October or November, the nearby trees spiky things – explosions of black twigs in shockwaves of yellow leaves. In the reality of late March it was overcast and threatening rain as I closed the cap on the toothpaste and caught my reflection in the mirror: my hairline receding, my jawline beginning to sag. A reminder – I am connected to time whether I like it or not. Place, however, is another matter. Places slip through my fingers. I started to keep a list of previous addresses a few years ago; they fill a good side of A4 now. I am itinerant, the perpetual outsider.

The church is a partial ruin, its face a line of blind arches. Windows are bereft of tracery, the scars of former walls raw and protruding. Inside there is a faint tang of incense, a leftover from the last service. Some of the tombs are missing pieces of carving; there are broken leaves and some heads have been sensitively replaced. If it's true, as Ralph Waldo Emerson wrote, that sculpture is only beautiful when it ceases to be comprehensible, the stone transitioning from 'that which is representable to the senses to that which is not', then Winchelsea church is an engine for the imagination.

Yesterday I walked to Collington Woods, a tiny island of birds in an otherwise deathly suburb. In the silent landscape of clipped shrubs and classic cars under tarpaulins and cast cement lions guarding driveways I was an intruder, following the curve of streets whose names conjured the phantoms of rural England: Tanglewood Coppice, Hawkhurst Way, Holm Oak Close. A footpath took me to the woods. After the airless streets, this miniature square of zealously pruned and managed saplings where it is impossible to get lost was a relief. Foolishly I thought that something here might help me start to write about the Green Man, but I'm not sure if he, or it, has anything to do with actual living trees or greenery at all. As I left I passed a worried-looking couple walking in the opposite direction. I overheard the man saying 'it's void' and the woman nodding in agreement.

The name 'Green Man' was first used in 1939 in an article by Lady Raglan – Julia Somerset – to describe the abundant medieval carvings in which leaves appear to grow out of the mouth of a human face, sometimes also through the nose or even the eyes. They are found in churches and cathedrals throughout Britain and Europe dating from the eleventh to the sixteenth centuries. Their heyday was the Gothic period during which they were carved on architectural features such as roof bosses, corbels, capitals, but also on tombs and fonts. Raglan's article, her only writing on the subject, would influence an entire generation of researchers. The naming

of this leaf mask entered the image into a contemporary narrative and gave it a host of new associations drawn from folklore and the twentieth-century revival of paganism. It quickly became shorthand for some kind of spiritual impulse, an image apparently without any baggage, and, for that reason, able to circulate freely in a secular world. So it grew into a symbol of our desire to connect with some spirit or other; of an unknown god of the diminished woodland; or a pagan fertility totem held captive by a landlocked Christianity. Or simply another invented tradition based around pubs and morris dancing and Mayday. Whatever you wanted. But the image is so strong it's easy to fall under its spell.

My journey here reminded me just how much Winchelsea is defined by water. Out of Hastings the railway line runs east along Brede Level, the floodplain of the River Brede, taking a curve to the northeast just before Winchelsea station. The only passenger to get off, I have to wait for the train to leave before I can cross the line, following the twists of Station Road around field boundaries and over a bridge before meeting the main road where it hairpins on the northern edge of the town. The original town on the coast was destroyed by the sea and rebuilt on higher ground in the thirteenth century. The name reflects this primary location, the suffix 'chelsea' from the Saxon word *chesil*, referring to a shingle beach or embankment, while 'Win' may derive from *gwent* – a level – perhaps the marshland behind the old town. On the Ordnance Survey map the contours of the new Winchelsea are circled by blank flatlands crossed by the blue lines of drainage ditches.

I have no particular link with the town. I didn't grow up or live here and am an infrequent visitor. But I am drawn here. I come when I can, chiefly to look at the fourteenth-century tomb sculpture, one of the highlights of the Decorated Gothic. In the south of England it must rank alongside the outstanding reredos at Christchurch Priory in Dorset and the west front at Exeter Cathedral in Devon. The Green Man looks out from within a trefoil in the centre of a tomb's canopy, a mask on the threshold between life and death. Two stems creep out of each side of his mouth. The leaves are oak and, befitting the period, realistically carved with delicate lines. Nonetheless their effect is otherworldly, encircling his head like floating weed in a lazy tide.

This last aspect – something about the leaves suggests breath, as if the Green Man is himself underwater – makes me think of another image, one further west, in the Devon village of Luppitt. I visited a few months ago; I've stuck some of the photos I took that day above my desk. Here he's carved on a font and is from a few hundred year earlier. Unlike the delicate features of the Winchelsea head the one at Luppitt is brutal, a square skull with a beak-like mouth and bulging eyes, only one of which has a pupil. There is no lower jaw. A line of square teeth poke into the air and beneath them a mass of foliage slumps out, a mess of unidentifiable leaf shapes that fill an entire side of the font and flop under their own weight like the body of a washed up jellyfish. If you could pick them up they would droop around your hand.

The Luppitt Green Man appears alongside several fantastic creatures: a monstrous double-headed dragon, one head at the end of its tail with rows of pointy teeth; a centaur holding a spear; two men hammering a spike into a disembodied skull; a scene in which an unidentifiable animal is hunted by other unidentifiable animals. The whole piece is unusual, spare, carved with spectacular vision. As at Winchelsea the Green Man is between states and beyond places, immersed in the world of the grotesque in which opposites combine, monsters are the norm and the world is turned upside down. It seems a fitting style to find in buildings that are themselves in-between one thing and another – sacred and profane, human and divine – and carved on items of religious furniture associated with rites of transition.

There is a chill in the air and I shiver. I am mindful of the time as there is a train only once every two hours. So I get up and, skimming the titles of books for sale on the way out, go and walk around the churchyard. There is a bench inside the ruined transept and I sit for a moment, sheltered from the breeze by the remaining section of wall. Ruins have always struck me as paradoxical, places where time is made visible in space through the processes of decay. 'Incomplete works have a greater power on the imagination' writes Timothy Walsh, referencing the twentieth-century artist Auguste Rodin's obsession with fragments. Ruins force us to enter the gap, complete the missing part. In these places we might find absent or wandering parts of ourselves.

When I became a stonemason one of the first things a friend asked me to carve was a Green Man. I was unconfident, as yet unaware that, as Carla Needleman writes, 'craftsmanship begins with disillusion'. The process of making something – that never quite becomes what you had imagined – was new to me and I interpreted it then as failure instead of the genuine gift of discovery it often is. I was tentative and approached the task slowly. I found

a suitable block of Portland stone and using clay made some macquettes to copy. But each time I modelled a Green Man the image seemed to escape me. Again and again. In the end I lost impetus and never carved the piece. But the project, abandoned as it was, nevertheless got me looking closely at the carvings, thinking about leaf shapes and the absence of roots. In particular the roots. Where were they?

There are some Green Man carvings where, in addition to leaves growing out of the mouth, they curl out of the eye sockets, the nostrils, or burst out of the skin, the implication being that this is a decaying corpse, the plant life growing through the body – entirely in keeping with its regular appearance on tombs. But for the most part these images are outnumbered by masks where the foliage grows from the mouth only, as at Winchelsea and Luppitt, divergent in style as these examples are. The roots, then, are within. The Green Man speaks in leaves but his words are not of the natural world: they are the shapes of darkness, a cuneiform of the unconscious. This is the life hidden from view by the body, a language of transitions and gaps, endings and beginnings; most crucially, perhaps, of connections that anchor us in the midst of the unknown. These are not connections with place, at least not primarily, but connections through time.

The Green Man stalks my own timeline in strange and elusive ways. He is the voice I can't quite hear and the face I don't fully see. He cannot move from his stone bed – I cannot quite approach it. Though I have been trying to, unconsciously perhaps, for most of my life. We are connected.

On the stone reredos or altar screen inside Christchurch Priory, about 140 miles west along the coast, there is a carving of a Tree of Jesse. This is a kind of family tree depicting the ancestors of Christ, intended to show his royal lineage and connections, however tenuous, with noble families. In the medieval period great emphasis was placed upon heredity, both for claiming mystical power and authority (some families claiming descent from mythical creatures such as mermaids, for example) and for the careful management and passing on of resources, chiefly land. Based on a passage from the Book of Isaiah, the tree grows out of Jesse of Bethlehem, the father of King David, its swirling branches connecting up the other figures.

I know Christchurch well, or at least I did in the eighties through regular visits to the town to see my aunt. Each time I became more and more interested in the architecture of the medieval priory and the nearby land by the river. The decorative Romanesque north transept; the fragments of the castle on its motte; the remains of the Constable's House; the marble mausolea whose desolate curves were accentuated by sympathetically planted trees. I took photographs of them all. I collected postcards of places that seemed unearthly too: St Catherine's Chapel at Abbotsbury in a thick morning mist, Long Bredy barrow at sunset.

Years later, as a stonemason at Exeter Cathedral, I worked conserving the medieval sculpture of the west front – carved by the same team of masons who'd made the screen at Christchurch. I'd been looking at their sculpture, made six hundred and seventy years earlier, since my teens. I discovered a stonemason ancestor,

also called Alexander, working the granites of Scotland in the eighteenth century. I had written a branch of my own Jesse Tree, or had been written by it, its obscure shoots sprouting up in places along the south coast: Winchelsea, Christchurch, Exeter.

'If this is your land, where are your stories?' asks an elder of a First Nations community in northwest British Columbia to the officials claiming the land for the government. 'All of a sudden', writes J. Edward Chamberlin, present at the scene, 'everyone understood … even though the government foresters didn't know a word of Gitskan, and neither did some of his Gitskan companions'. I realise I've forgotten to leave a donation so I get up and go back inside the church. The light has softened with the afternoon and the stone tombs appear muted and restful. The Green Man has sunk back into his background, relinquishing the sharp shadows of earlier. I drop some noisy coins into the box. Maybe the Green Man is the guardian of these invisible maps, the maps that can't be drawn in two dimensions, the threads that connect us across time to other people and places and so help to make sense of our own times and places. His roots, if anywhere, are, like our own, inside. In the dark. In the blood and the nerve endings and the gut instinct. In the line that stretches back to who has come before. In what and who you love. They are nourished by the stories we tell about all these things, stories that can be fixed in places outside the body, that connect the inner and outer worlds. For, as Chamberlin noted, moved by the encounter between native and official, every story 'brings the imagination and reality together in moments of what we might as well call faith'.

Today is Lady Day, March 25, which until the mid-eighteenth century was the start of the new year. The grass is lit with daffodils and primroses. There are flecks of green on some of the trees. The sludgy days of early January are a distant memory. 'Cut a chrysalis open', writes Pat Barker in her novel *Regeneration*, 'and you will find a rotting caterpillar'. Transformation, she concludes, 'consists almost entirely of decay'. As I leave I realise that that's probably why I've been drawn here this afternoon, to a semi-ruinous church. To reconnect with something intangible and unknowable, the processes of change themselves and the stories that help us negotiate them. All, perhaps, crystallised in the face of the Green Man.

On my journey back I have to change trains in Hastings. There is a fifty-minute wait, so I walk into town for a drink. My route takes me past a second-hand record shop. They are playing The Smiths. There is a good selection of almost everything you might want, from reggae to post-punk. I find a section of seven-inch singles labelled 'Gothic/Synthpop', a pairing I've not encountered before but of course, why not, it makes perfect sense. I flick through the records. Siouxsie and the Banshees, The Cure, New Order, as I'd expect. But Duran Duran? Here it is, the first record I ever bought, the thread-like root out of which an unusual plant grew. Its title is, amusingly, a question I've been asking myself a lot lately: 'Is There Something I Should Know?' From the back of my mind the quizzical face of the Winchelsea Green Man, in his ambient ruff of oak leaves, looks on. ✪

ON RED HAIR
AND BELONGING

ROUTES OF ANCESTRY AND MIGRATION

Words: Catherine Mitchell
Illustration: Lucy Eldridge

The genetics of red hair are as complex as its colourful origin myths. We untangle the layers of intuitive association connecting supernatural beings, bloodthirsty warriors and sensitive souls.

I'm young. I don't remember exactly how old. I'm standing on a small square landing halfway up the stairs at my grandmother's house, a tiny wooden stool on my right. On the stool are three minute terracotta vases. They are grey-blue with a shell-like lustre, probably only a centimetre or two high. Tiny vases for tiny flowers. On the left of the stool, in front of me and hanging on the wall, is a giant mirror framed with dark wood and gilt. In the mirror a young girl looks back at me. She's the same age and height as me, yet her skin is fair and freckly, her hair a bright copper. I peer closer and so does she. And as the light bends back and forth between us, a quiet realisation starts to settle – this is me and this is what I look like, on the outside, to others. And this is significant. Significant enough to burrow a permanent little place into my memory, for up until that moment I had, on the inside, without realising, looked just like my best friend – with darker skin, long dark hair and no freckles.

I have no recollections of the hours or weeks surrounding that moment. It hangs all by itself, like a single painting in a small room of a gallery. As though it were part of an exhibition – the history of me. What I can't tell you however is how accurate that story is. My grandmother did have the tiny vases, a mirror on the landing and I did realise at that moment that I looked different from the image in my mind. But how much did the red hair stand out back then from any other feature? Or has its importance been accentuated over the years, layers upon layers of pigment, one for each reflection, colour-tinting the memory like a vintage photograph? And for each layer, a deepening realisation that it was a thing to have red hair. That it signified difference. That it signified as many different things as you care to imagine.

I was always told from childhood that red hair is recessive, only popping up in families where both parents carry a gene. I'm no geneticist. The genetics are, I understand, more nuanced and complex, yet I was certainly a surprise. After a little investigation, my parents discovered a shared redheaded ancestry four generations back. A great-grandmother on each side with red hair – genes that had lain dormant for generations, until I came screaming into the world with a bright coppery mane. Discovered in 1995, MC1R or the melanocortin 1 receptor, sits on chromosome 16 and is responsible for our ability to tan. It responds to and protects us from the effects of strong sun by producing eumelanin. Strong eumelanin production results in dark hair, skin and eyes, good sun protection – my childhood friend. Most people with red hair (but not all – there are various genetics at play for other groups with red hair, such as those in the Solomon Islands) will have a variant of the MC1R which produces much less eumelanin and more pheomelanin, resulting in red hair, pale skin and freckles, less tanning ability and far less protection from the damaging effects of the sun.

So how could this genetic quirk have survived, and in some areas flourished? There is a theory. In 2010, genetics student Emily Pritchard's PhD thesis suggested that rather than placing the redhead at a disadvantage, the variant in the MC1R gene gave the carrier a distinct advantage in northern climates where the sun was weak. Jacky Colliss Harvey, in her book, *Red: A Natural History of the Redhead*, takes us back to when the ice began to retreat around 20,000 years ago and people started migrating north and west, from Russia into Scandinavia and northwest Europe. Here, individuals with this genetic variant found themselves naturally suited to the gloomy skies and weaker light. Low eumelanin allows the body to be much more efficient at absorbing vitamin D in low light conditions. Vitamin D is crucial for creating strong bones and a deficiency can lead to the crippling effect of rickets. In women, it could result in a contorted pelvis, making child-birth life-threatening. 'Which,' Colliss Harvey ponders, 'along with all the other ancient and instinctive associations of the color red (fire, blood, passion, ripeness) does rather open the question as to whether the often highly sexualized image of female redheads might not start here, with the simple fact that choosing a redhead as a mate meant you bred successfully and that your pale-skinned children, … did the same.' In a tiny footnote, she tells us that an old gypsy amulet for successful childbirth was to sew a lock of red hair into a bag and wear it next to the belly during pregnancy.

There is evidence of red hair (along with a range of other hair colours similar to those found today) as far back as the Paleolithic period in Europe. In 2007, DNA was extracted from Neanderthal remains containing a variant of the MC1R gene which would have caused red hair in those who carried it. However further research found that it wasn't the same variant that exists today. And rather than being our ancestors, Neanderthals are now strongly thought to have reached an evolutionary dead end, dying out between 28,000 and 24,000 years ago.

Modern statistics and mapping of red hair seem to be somewhat lacking in verifiable sources, yet there is a general pattern – the further north and west into Europe you go, the higher the percentage of redheads. A pattern, it has been suggested, that correlates with the ancient Celtic and Germanic worlds.

Scotland is usually cited as the place with the most redheads, with around thirteen percent of the overall population having red hair, around three times as many as in England. Ireland comes in second with some ten percent of the population having red hair. One origin myth takes us to Ireland, where the twelfth-century *Lebor Gabála Érenn*, *The Book of Invasions*, tells stories of the Tuath Dé Danann, a mythical race with supernatural powers who are said to have arrived in Ireland on flying ships on dark clouds. They were treated as gods or beings from another world. We are told that, in comparison to the small, darker skinned native Irish, they looked startlingly different, being tall and pale with red or blonde hair, and blue or green eyes. (As with many ancient stories of red hair, it seems that specific nuances of tone, for example between red and blonde, or green or blue, has been lost in translation down the ages). *The Annals of the Four Masters*, chronicles of medieval Irish history compiled by Franciscan monks in the seventeenth century, say the Danann ruled pre-Christian Ireland from 1897 to 1700BC until defeated by the Milesians, an early Gaelic tribe. The Danann were forced into the underworld where they became the fair, or fairy folk.

The Danann are said to have hailed from the mythical cities of the north: Murias, Gorias, Falias and Finias in Lochlann, modern-day Norway. Which brings us (with a recessive hop and a skip) to the Vikings some 3,000 years later. 'If you look at where the red-haired patterning is in Ireland, in particular, it is very much around the areas where Vikings settled,' Professor Donna Heddle of the University of the Highlands and Islands' Centre for Nordic Studies has said. But what about the Celts who were already in central Europe and Britain and had been for over a millennium, since around 500BC? We know that Scottish Celts were taken, possibly as slaves, to southwest Norway by the Vikings, and that the frequency of red hair increased there as a result. However, the origin of red hair is now thought to be not in Scotland, Ireland or even northwest Europe, but the ancient Tocharian tribe in the Tarim Basin in what is now the Xinjiang Province, China. Here, four-thousand-year-old mummies have been excavated and examined and found to have red and blonde hair from the same MC1R variant that exists today. It's thought pockets of redheads were distributed throughout Asia, Russia and Europe via that ancient trading route, the Silk Road.

I'm now five or six. My parents have just returned from parents' evening and I'm getting a firm talking-to. My teacher thinks I am a troublemaker. My parents do not. Instead they are convinced that I have been picked out on account of my hair. I will need to be careful, to not draw attention to myself. Almost a decade later they refuse to allow me to attend protest marches in London. They believe I will be arrested. Not because of my behaviour, but because, being a redhead, I will stand out. I defy them. Attend the rallies. Do not get arrested. And I can, to this day, find no evidence of redheads having greater arrest statistics than non-redheads.

But were my parents on to something? Redheads throughout history have had a reputation, it seems, for fiery tempers and causing trouble. The Celts and Vikings are both described as bloodthirsty, violent tribes. As are the Thracians, dating back 3,000 years in what is today Bulgaria, Turkey and Greece. They were often described as ferocious barbarians, bloodthirsty warriors, and worshippers of Dionysus. Roman chronicler Livy described how their battle songs, their howling and leaping, and their appearance with 'long red hair', were 'designed to terrify'.

In Urdmurtia today, a region on the Volga river in central Russia, there remains a hotspot of redheads, more than ten percent of the population, a frequency only found elsewhere in Ireland and Scotland. The Udmurt people have been described as 'the most redheaded men in the world', while their ancient relatives, the Budini people, a Scythian tribe, were noted for their fiery hair and violence by the Greek historian, Herodotus.

The power of red hair to arouse fear is a recurrent theme. In Ancient Egypt, redheaded men were burnt alive and their ashes offered to Osiris, god of corn and the underworld. We also find tales of Cleopatra being a redhead. Unlike with Rameses II, however, it seems there is little evidence to back this up beyond henna being fashionable at the time. Collis Harvey suggests instead that these stories were propaganda, using hair colour to invoke a personality rather than an appearance, asking rhetorically about her hair, 'what other color would it be?'.

In a similar way, Boudicca is often described as tall with a mass of red hair, yet Roman historian, Cassius Dio, writing 100 or so years after her death, uses the word *xanthotatos*, to describe her hair, meaning very yellow or tawny, a yellowy-brown, rather than red. Children's author of the Roman Mysteries series, Caroline Lawrence, suggests rather than being an accurate reflection of the physical colour of her hair, it's an accurate reflection of the emotions this colour would have had for the Romans. *Xanthotatos* would also have brought to mind 'gold, sand, corn, bile and lions'. She suggests that, on an emotional level, 'red' today has a similar feeling to the fierce, dangerous, lion-like qualities of 'tawny' in Roman times. The Urban Dictionary defines red hair as 'A rare natural hair colour which inspires odd and sometimes fearful reactions from the more common coloured hair types,' while *The Penguin Guide to Superstitions* identifies a 'general prejudice … that red-haired people are devious, cruel, lascivious, unlucky and generally untrustworthy.' Judas Iscariot is the redheaded symbol of betrayal. A strong emotional response to redheads certainly lingers today. While in the US, the term 'ginger' is not considered derogatory and red hair is cherished, it is still derided in northern Europe and in particular in the UK, despite the high number of redheads. Bullying is rife and public abuse from the playground to the airwaves is sadly commonplace. Is it any wonder we redheads are labelled sensitive?

I'm in my early 20s and I'm about to have a general anaesthetic for the first time. I'm having my wisdom teeth removed. The anaesthetist holds my hand, chuckles and tells me I'll need more anaesthetic as I'm a redhead. I start to wonder if he's joking and then everything goes black.

Years later I wake up screaming in agony after emergency surgery to have my appendix removed. I'm in Uganda. I try to explain to the nurse, in my delirious state, that I'm a redhead and need more pain relief, but I'm probably far from coherent. Writhing in pain, a nurse gives me a wooden dowel to bite down on. He holds my hand and gives me a local name from the Nkima (Monkey) clan, his own. He explains I have earned it, as though I have passed through a fire of initiation. I appreciate the gesture. I really appreciate the analgesic when it is finally offered.

Three years later and on another operating table, this time after the emergency caesarean birth of my daughter, I am told everything had gone very well. I nod, relieved. They explain that, on account of my hair colour, they were expecting me to haemorrhage. A 2006 peer-reviewed paper in *Anesthesia & Analgesia* found no increased risk of post-operative bleeding for redheads, although they did acknowledge a slight increase in bruising, yet bizarrely this seems to be a myth that medical professionals stand by.

Having often wondered if there's anywhere I would feel a sense of belonging, where my hair would not be an issue, I visit Glasgow for the first time. Aged 22, it is the furthest north and west I have so far travelled. I'm vaguely attentive as I walk down Sauchiehall Street at midday, but there's an almost dreamlike quality to my surroundings, a deja-vu. Something familiar and comfortable. And then I see them. Redheads. Everywhere. People who look like me and in reassuring numbers. I realise, for the first time in my life, that I don't stand out.

Today I wonder again whether, if you placed a true snapshot of that moment next to my memory there would have been far fewer redheads there than I recollect. Having recently relocated with my family to the west coast of Scotland I have to admit that, despite the statistics, I have not noticed a greater percentage of redheads here than elsewhere.

In 2007, stories abounded in the press foretelling the extinction of red hair in response to climate change. The DNA testing company behind the data was later discredited and there is no evidence that red hair is set to die out (or that Scotland will become any sunnier). For a while I dyed my hair. First bright red and then blonde. Eventually I noticed my natural copper had started to fade. Today, in some lights, people don't always realise that I am a redhead. They may say something offhand about redheads before slowing, hesitating, catching my real hair colour. Perhaps I am becoming less attuned as I get older and less red. ✪

AN HOUR TO SING

A JOURNEY OF FOLLOWING

Poet: Kym Martindale
Artist: Caroline Blythe

In 1913, writer Edward Thomas was on the brink of becoming a poet; Europe was on the brink of world war, the conflict in which Thomas would die, three years later. That year however, Thomas cycled from London to Somerset, to find spring, and wrote of the journey in In Pursuit of Spring. Pursuit – the chase, the hunt, but also the occupation, the concern.

Between 2012-2017, poet and cyclist Kym Martindale began the pursuit of Edward Thomas, riding and writing Thomas's route. In 2014, she and Thomas were joined by artist Caroline Blythe. Joined? Yes, they were a gang, but singing their own parts, as Kym chased Thomas's spirit, and Caroline followed Kym. Poet and artist found not spring, not Thomas, but endless resonances, as poems, images, layers circled restlessly. And this was as good as finding Thomas, or spring.

What did the thrushes know? Rain, snow, sleet, hail,
Had kept them quiet as the primroses.
They had but an hour to sing. On boughs they sang,
On gates, on ground; they sang while they changed perches
And while they fought, if they remembered to fight;
So earnest were they to pack into that hour
Their unwilling hoard of song

From 'March'
Edward Thomas, 1914

1913: Edward Thomas, travel writer, cyclist and walker, naturalist, essayist, biographer and – but not yet – poet, takes a journey on a bicycle. 2012: I decide to follow.

1913: the season is Easter, a March Easter, and the journey from London to the Quantocks, in Somerset, is recorded in *In Pursuit of Spring*. 1913, and Thomas seeks Spring, yes; he noses his way towards light and warmth, regeneration; but like me, he also seeks a poet: 'I would see Nether Stowey,' he writes, 'the native soil of 'Kubla Khan'.'

The poetry and the poet are significant for *In Pursuit of Spring* was Thomas's swansong to prose, but this prose is turned like loam in preparation, scattered with the poems he has yet to write. 'Wales very far off,' he notes on Cothelstone Hill, Somerset, a 'blueness' glimpsed through a 'low-arched rainbow'. Thomas was of Welsh descent, loved and visited the country often, and wrote about it in *Beautiful Wales* (1905). The wistful blueness, very far off, marks his horizon like the poetry he will write from 1914 until his death at Arras in 1917; so, *In Pursuit of Spring* snakes like Offa's Dyke between Thomas the jobbing writer, and Thomas, poet – at last. Offa's Dyke traces old borders and ancient anxieties. *In Pursuit of Spring* crosses seasons and counties but, like spring itself, cradles return in lines, cadences and images that will bloom differently in poems like 'March'.

I think I might catch his essence. I think the hedgerows, hills and fields are bound to give him up; if I can see what he saw, something of the man might be recovered. But it is not immediate, and it is never certain. I snatch days here and there, matching miles where and when I can. I make notes en route, take pictures, and the poems follow, not immediately, but sometimes certain. And Caroline follows me. This is a project of following. She takes my material: notes, sections of OS maps, and extracts from Thomas with grid references scribbled in the margins. She finds her own moments, retraces my traces, draws and re-draws, then interleaves actual tracings of parts of each sketch. She layers our responses: mine to Thomas, hers to Thomas and my poems – we are re-making something together, separately. The drawings take on their own architecture, and we both enjoy how, where scholars and historians want to peel away time, here we are, piling up palimpsests as we go.

So, this is the poetry, visual and written, of journeys. The seasons are various, the travellers are curious. The journeys are incomplete.

Aren't they always.

1913: it is a March Easter, and unsettled, but Thomas must stitch his heart to his chosen hour of going.

'Whatever happened, I was to start on Good Friday'

The next day was sleet. […] I did not forget Easters of
snow and of north wind. In the end I decided to trust to luck
— to start on Good Friday on the chance that I should meet
fine weather at once or in a day or two.
In Pursuit of Spring

Throughout the month the distribution of atmospheric
pressure round the British Isles was of a very unsettled type.
Monthly Weather Report Of The Meteorological
Office: No. 111. March 1913

He was to start on Good Friday.
Throughout March, the distribution of atmospheric pressure made a noise
as if the earth were hollow and rumbling;
numerous depressions wandered along very irregular paths, and all day
with a rhythmless roar scoured the earth like a pot. Snow fell,
thin as rice after a wedding, while rough and boisterous the wind
was eager to scour old men, infants, and celandines.

These were days of great rather than of little things, velocities
of 75 and 69 miles per hour at Pendennis and Kew; Worthing pier was destroyed
by the wind that was cleaning, and an earth tremor was felt in the world that
was being cleaned and he was to start on Good Friday.

For most of one day it rained; what was done under cover
of that day only a poet can tell: precipitation everywhere in excess, there being
an entire absence of man or god, more trees and flowers than children,
an earlier than prehistoric day.
18.1 inches of rain,
19.3 inches of rain,
and generally the frequency exceeding 28 days in many places.
But on Good Friday, he would start.

Under cover of that deliberate, irresistible rain, the sun rose glimmeringly
and a blackbird sang as if the world were his nest.
The early morning of the 18th was marked by sharp frost, the wind cold,
and light died utterly.
On the morning of the 22nd a large disturbance disembowelled
the universe, and thunder fell with a single
plunge and rebound as of an enormous weight.

As deeply as one pearl dropped over Southern England where the force
of a whole gale was felt
was that planet lost in the night.
Even if the sun went down in peace, what of the morrow? For whatever happened, he had to
start on the next day.
Good Friday.

Prologue
Summer 2012:

At first, the bike is the point, you see. I like Thomas's poetry, but I love cycling. Finding *In Pursuit of Spring* is brilliant because I can chase a poet on a bike. Research cannot get better than this.

I also love birds, and here is Thomas, listening to his first chiffchaff on Easter Saturday, 1913, at Froyle, Hampshire. It sings, he thinks 'more shrilly than usual, something distractedly.' But he is satisfied. It has the 'least of songs' he says, but he goes 'on more cheerfully, as if each note had been a hammering of a tiny nail into Winter's coffin.'

Spring has come and will 'not be repulsed'. Every year he listens and notes the date of the first chiffchaff's song, and it is always close to March 19.

The frailty of birdsong is its assurance and apprehension. The return of swifts, for instance, their swooping screams at first so faint you think you imagine it from desiring it so. The marvel of the swift is that it seems to materialise from the sky, taking earthly form every year in honour of some ancient promise. I wrote a poem about this before I knew about Ted Hughes's 'Swifts'.

Chiff-Chaff

It was here, and at eleven, that I first heard the chiffchaff saying, "chiff-chaff, chiff-chaff, chiff-chaff, chiff!" ... the small bird's double note almost as regular as the ticking of a clock [...] sounded very clear in the coomb. [...] I always expect him and always hear him.

In Pursuit of Spring

the least of songs / shrill distracted / this least of songs /nails winter down / the least of songs / tap tap / tick tock / the least of songs beats out spring's stride – not a song /a search for song / half a crotchet twice/ chiff-chaff and then /chiff chiff-chaff chiff/this least of songs but first of songs

marches out for March

Between Winchester and Salisbury
July 2012:

Interval: the year has a score, and Thomas reads it, hears it, plays it back to us. The lanes and hedges are staves, and the birds cram them; the sky waits for them to scrawl across it, signing off summer, autumn, spring.

The yellowhammer has nothing clarion about it, unlike the chiffchaff or swift. Thomas calls it the 'sleepiest-voiced' of birds. It underscores summer nevertheless, and it is the leitmotif of my first tracing.

But, Caroline frets at not hearing it, anxiously checking the quiet air, for at least its grace notes.

Yellowhammer

The ways of such a road – when the June grass is high and in the sun it is invisible, except for its blueness and its buttercups, and the chaffinch, the corn-bunting, and the yellow-hammer, the sleepiest-voiced birds are most persistent – easily persuade the mind that it alone is travelling, travelling through an ideal country, belonging to itself and beyond the power of the world to destroy.

Heart Of England, 1906

In a measure of swift crotchets,
    stuttered sweetly,
All day he begs begs begs
    for no-cheeeeeese.

The hammer
  tiny and sharp
of his cry,
raps at the gutstring taut
across the season's chamber
    as hollow as his coda
the long   resigned   plea
of the breve.

The yellowhammer's masterstroke
  to sound summer's minor key
  to insist its fragility
  in counterpoint to the complexity
of leaf, harvest and song
his last cadence as long as blank fields,
  bowls and mouths.

On the Plain:
Salisbury and Thereabouts, August 2015

Interval: I ride easily enough to Stapleford, to join Thomas there. Already there is a languor in the air that tastes of old summers, as if the past might be around the next bend. It almost could: Thomas describes contours, ridges, and copses so precisely that you can see them, if they still exist. But the seven hares playing follow-my-leader on Crouch's Down are long gone, and only Thomas saw them.

And the bike is no longer the point. I am on a countdown to April 2017, and mortality is nudging hard. His. Ergo, mine. Ergo, disappointment. In Stapleford Church, there is a brass plaque to the vicar's son, who drowned at Porthcurno in 1908. My pencil notes: he missed the trenches, though. A strange grief creeps alongside, like a shadow I cannot lose. In a pamphlet about the village's history, there is a photograph of a young man c.1910; he is dressed from head to foot in furs, in the cottage garden of his family who lived in Stapleford. He smiles quietly from the enormous hood of his outfit, the rest of him lost to the furs. Incongruously, pathetically, he also wears a little muffler. This is Gilbert Scott who went with the other Scott (no relation) to the Antarctic, and survived to die at Gallipoli instead. I imagine him paused in the garden here, perhaps on Easter Sunday morning weighing the day's rainclouds against the brutality of the South Pole, the madness of the other Scott, the unease in Europe. And Thomas wheeling past, just out of view. But stopping, as he does, to read the gravestones in Stapleford Church yard.

Caroline's pencil shades in the graves, gently. This was a dark section, she said. So, the shadow followed her, too.

This Observation

The church is kept open, a clean, greenish place with
Norman arches […] The lettering survived on the headstone
of John Saph, who died in 1683, and his wife, Alice, who
died in 1677.

In Pursuit of Spring

Three hundred years and counting,
mill at the shoulders of this observation,
days of rain and dust, sun and wind,
months of reading and forgetting,
centuries of scouring
and worshipping.

This observation hunches against
so many others, which gather
and poke awkwardly at the power
of words and stone
over the soft hostage of the body.

For example, between his gaze
and his notes, the soil slips through
the claw of ribs,
a metatarsal is nudged aside by moles,
while silk and wool cling airlessly
to bone
while cheeks and bellies
sink.

For example, his pencil shudders
at the chill of earth clattering
smothering,
and recognizes the anguish
of fragility understood.

Nether Stowey, the Quantocks, March 2013

Interval: the strangest day, the coldest day, the loneliest. What am I doing?

It may be the iron-grey bitterness of the weather, but I feel the point of all this dulling into absurdity. In the 'Hood Arms' on the A39, where Thomas spent a night, I wait for my partner to collect me. There are old photographs in the bar, and I look carefully – just in case. The place is disturbing. Old hunting jackets and leggings hang on nails from beams, but I am the only customer. It is as if the hunt came in, undressed and vanished. The jackets and leggings are frosted with dust and cobwebs. At Nether Stowey, a few miles away, Coleridge's cottage has been re-created to look as if the poet and his family are due back from a walk at any moment. A kind of sob sits on my chest.

Thomas was never happily married. He once said that he should have lived alone, but lacked the courage, that it was the kindness and love of his wife and children that made 'life almost impossible.'

What are we doing, hunting poets through cracks in time? Hauling traces, all of us, out of slipstreams.

Later, Caroline tells me that she harnessed help with this section, a friend who drove her in my wake. It was highly efficient she said, but sheer in its focus, and history, fugitive.

At Midnight

[T]he abounding honeysuckle produced an effect of wildness and richness, purity and softness, so vivid that the association of Nether Stowey was hardly needed to summon up Coleridge. The mere imagination of what these banks would be like when the honeysuckle was in flower was enough to suggest the poet. I became fantastic, and said to myself that the honeysuckle was worthy to provide the honeydew for nourishing his genius[.]

In Pursuit of Spring

The wind bowls the hapless moon,
bumping it over the seam of midnight,
      And it flares its silly surprise at the jolt.

I sit, listen, watch.
The scoured hills, the bleached fields stripped of time
      offer no clutter to warm or distract.

Then *they* seem close,
      scratching out poems in the cold,
      fingers and eyes numb from being pressed up
to the landscape,
      shoulders hunched against all need
but their own,
      which clawed grimly at their throats.

A century ago, a poet to be walks out,
      his pocket alive with intention,
      hand curled/uncurled,
      damp round the gun's barrel.
But there are poems to be written,
as the air knows, and refuses
to open for his falling body—
                    yet.

Two centuries away, an owl seals the night's stillness,
twice,
and a poet
tenderly cloaks his sleeping son in
crags and skies,
filling the child's formless dreams
with wishes.
In the years to come, his own dreams
shake him off
spiralling upwards on their great wings,
poised to stoop at the first glint

of promise,
though he voyages in
desperately
decreasing circles.

A hundred years ago (more or less)
poetry shoves its fist — hard
      into the small of his back;
      he can hear the words crunching,
      as tough and frail as bird bones,
      words choosing him, gathering
      like starlings at dusk, scrawls of them
      busy in – what he feels, nevertheless – to be
      his sunset. I watch and listen. Time heals itself
and the moon spins on towards a lighter sky;
the chaos of tomorrow and tomorrow
is already bullying at the door and clutter
blooms across the hills, the fields, the shock
of its return hollowing out this horizon.

The consolation is not theirs, but ours.
      As the Team's Head Brass
        Kubla Khan
          Adelstrop
             Frost at Midnight

at midnight
    time closes the wound.

KYM MARTINDALE and CAROLINE BLYTHE

Cothelstone Hill, March 1913/2013

I had found Spring, and I was confident that I could
ride home again and find Spring all along the road.

In Pursuit of Spring

The past is another country and it is warmer there.
The past is another country, a tidy century away.
This past is a country with no world war yet,

and no war poets; Prufrock, Bloom, cenotaphs, poppies,
yet to happen,
form and reason strangely alien in new hands.

The present was unborn, unthinkable, but
fumbled its way out of history all the same.

The hope for Cothelstone Hill to straddle the centuries,
for gorse to burn still like flames sown by the sun, for the planet
to tilt us again into the warmth and light, for the seasons to bring us their signs

and tributes – as they did apparently for him; the hope knows its
hubris, but seizes the signs anyway.
I walk up Cothelstone Hill with conceits in my heart –

the seeking and finding of resolve and spring, gathered and left on the grave of winter;
the world relinquishing Thomas to me;
the telling of the thing for the doing of the thing.

I walk up the hill, pretty consolations grinding like pebbles
in my notebook, for I am stalking a dead man;
I am haunting and haunted.

I walk up the hill like a lover
with relish in the drama of the differences,
the more stark the better. He has sun, rainbows, bouquets;
I have hoar frost and irony.

I have come north for Thomas, from a Cornwall
silly with catkins, daffodils and incipient green; the plot thickens as
I tumble back from March to January, as he bounds from March to May;

As he sits in the sun on Cothelstone Hill
on the last day of his journey westward
to find Spring, and Winter's grave, and dreams

of cowslips, cuckoos, rosemary and crown-imperial lining his way home,
I pass by, ice and frost cracking underfoot.
We nod in complicity.

April 1913 saw heavy snowfalls and cold resurrection; Thomas researched
his journey, with companions, over several months;
our quests meet in their desires.

Yes, the past is another country, far and near together.
The past is another country, but forlorn for a hand
to write it, direct it. Like us.

Epilogue

August 2015: it is so perfect, how the sign for Adlestrop is suddenly there, so unwonted, you might say. The lane is quiet, and the village itself nearly missed, but reversing, I see it: the railway bench from the old station, where no trains ever stop unwontedly or not. The poem is on a plaque on the bench.

The village hall is new, very slick. It is so slick that I don't make a donation to park there.

Adlestrop… sounds German, doesn't it?

Adlestrop

Adlestrop – honeyed to perfection
        cosying up to its poem.

Here Jane Austen occasionally stayed
        where Thomas never visited
        but remembered.

Here tennis parties and the country house
        are supreme, but the silence
        ticks as the heat ticks.

No-one coughs. I buy an ice-cream,
in the deeply quiet post office
and eat it on the church wall.

Little bird-song either. Someone arrives
to clean the church. The air re-gathers
in her wake.

No-one else comes. Or goes.

The poem's shadow falls everywhere: the railway bench
enshrined; endless postcards in the post office;

and Lob's Cottage at the foot of the hill.

Lob's Cottage.
It was after he died someone named it that.
But the gesture——

Little bird-song at this time of year. Woodpigeons,
goldfinches, swallows.
A robin.

And the train, its long rattle hastening the hour. ☻

ABANDONED MINES

THE WORK OF ENGINEER, KEITH RUSS

Interview: Jay Armstrong
Digital Modelling: Keith Russ

Over 25 years, Keith Russ has created three-dimensional maps of more than 350 abandoned mines around the world. The project began in the final year of his degree at Camborne School of Mines, now part of Exeter University, when he collaborated with Falmouth School of Art to build rudimentary animations of mines. Seeing the potential, he continued working on this for his PhD, starting by modelling South Crofty mine in Camborne, Cornwall.

A quarter of a century on he has mapped deserted mines from the Levant mine near Lands End, Cornwall to the Homestake mine in South Dakota, once the deepest gold mine in North America. These three-dimensional models of abandoned mines reveal the scale of what lies hidden in the earth and bear witness to the thousands of hours work of generations of miners who have shaped our modern world.

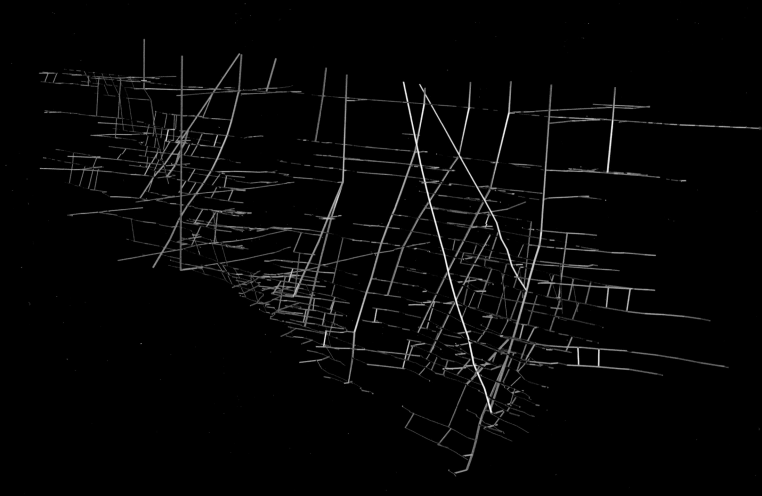

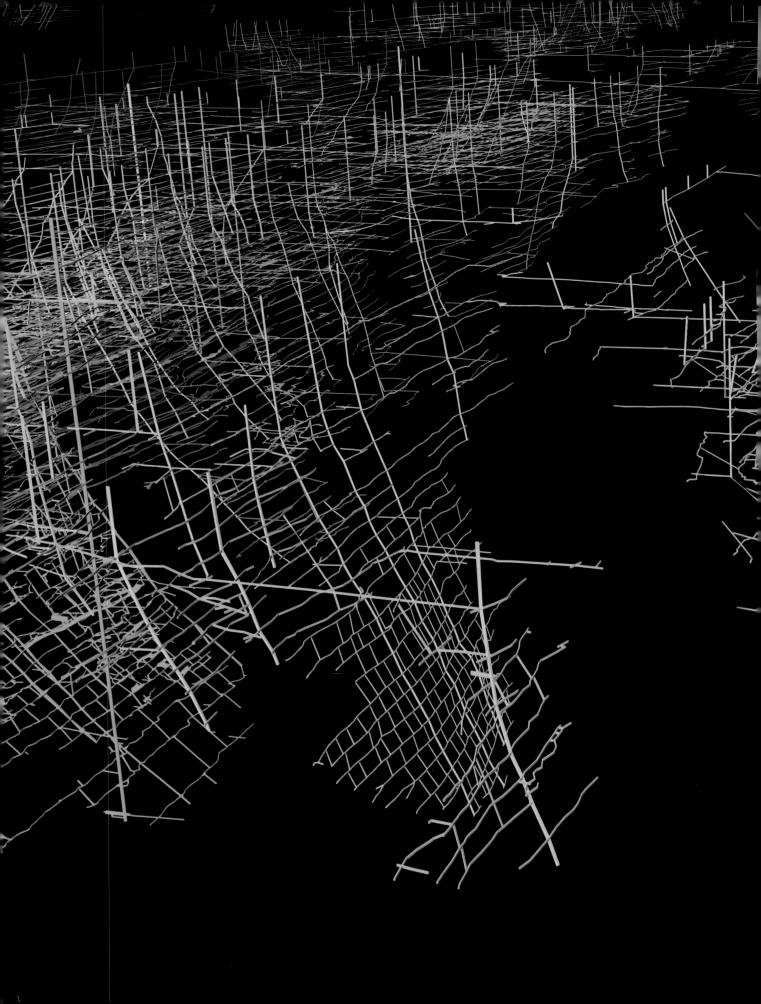

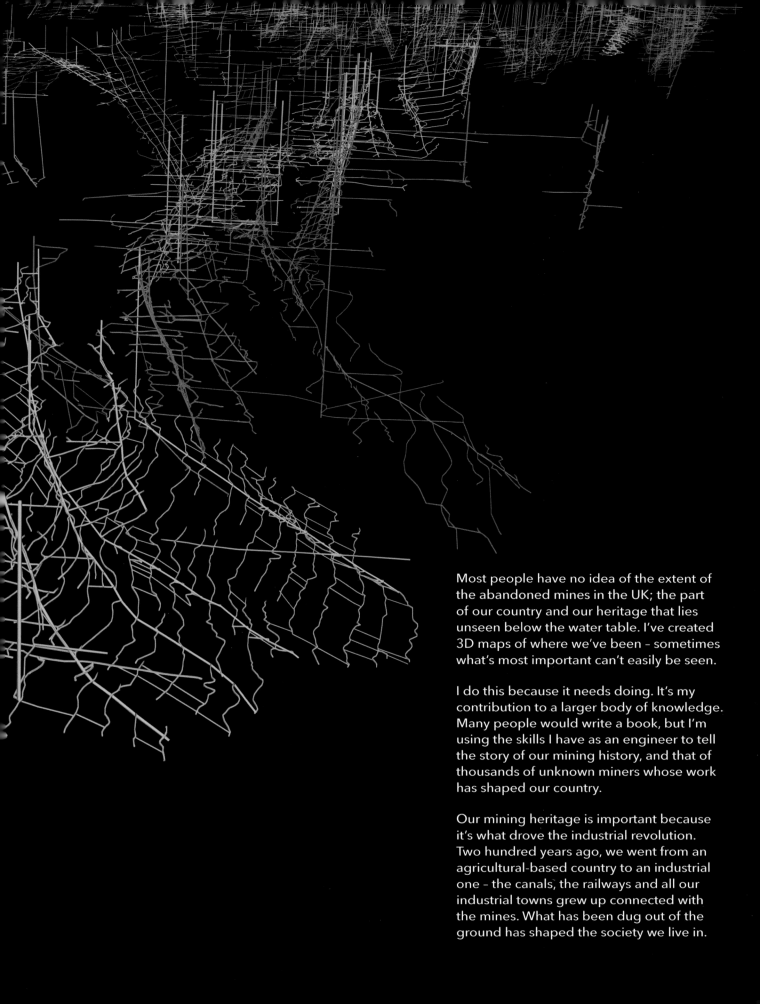

Most people have no idea of the extent of the abandoned mines in the UK; the part of our country and our heritage that lies unseen below the water table. I've created 3D maps of where we've been – sometimes what's most important can't easily be seen.

I do this because it needs doing. It's my contribution to a larger body of knowledge. Many people would write a book, but I'm using the skills I have as an engineer to tell the story of our mining history, and that of thousands of unknown miners whose work has shaped our country.

Our mining heritage is important because it's what drove the industrial revolution. Two hundred years ago, we went from an agricultural-based country to an industrial one – the canals, the railways and all our industrial towns grew up connected with the mines. What has been dug out of the ground has shaped the society we live in.

The process is fairly simple. Mine abandonment plans are available from the Public Records Office and I ask survey teams for the data. By digitising the plans, I can scale them to an Ordnance Survey (OS) map. The shafts on the mine model plan are then moved to fit the same locations on the map and I scale everything so their elevations are correct and they fit relative to each other.

I input this into a modelling package, fleshing it out so the model has a tunnel shape to it, and then I import them into an animation package. From this I can create a fly-through which I can easily sit and watch for hours.

What takes me maybe an hour or so now would have taken several months to do back in the early 1990s.

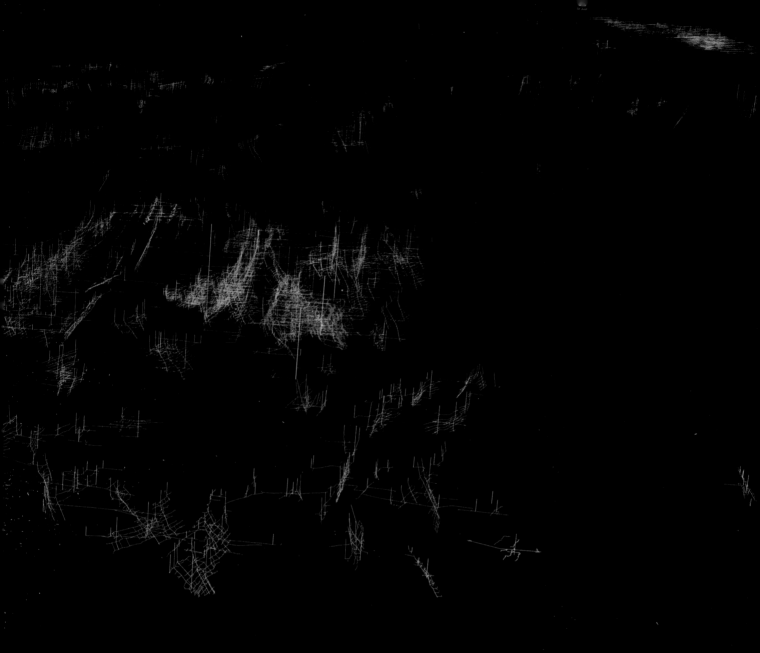

Historically, miners would have found the ore on the surface and followed it down, or found something in the cliffs, usually from colour variation, and followed it in. The wiggly passages in most of the old workings are from miners following the fracture in the rock which contains the tin or the copper. It would either run out or it wasn't worth going any further. Now we use a lot of drilling and a lot of geophysics and engineering – some of the passages are driven in where the material is, others are inserted in straight lines, from where the miners access the seams at an angle.

I once gave a talk and a group of retired miners came along. They had created some of the passages that are on the model. It was really good for them to see where they had spent the majority of their working life. They said it gave them some idea of perspective and told me they had worked in many different parts of the mine but only saw for the first time on the model how the levels related to each other.

This gave me an enormous sense of satisfaction. The models are abstract but they are based on something that's real – the holes are actually there, under the ground, and these miners created them. I was told about three generations of the same family who had worked in this mine. To think of the number of hours that have gone into creating these passages is just phenomenal. Mining is unseen but it's one of the world's oldest and most dangerous professions. Many lives were lost down these mines and it's not something we should forget. ≫→

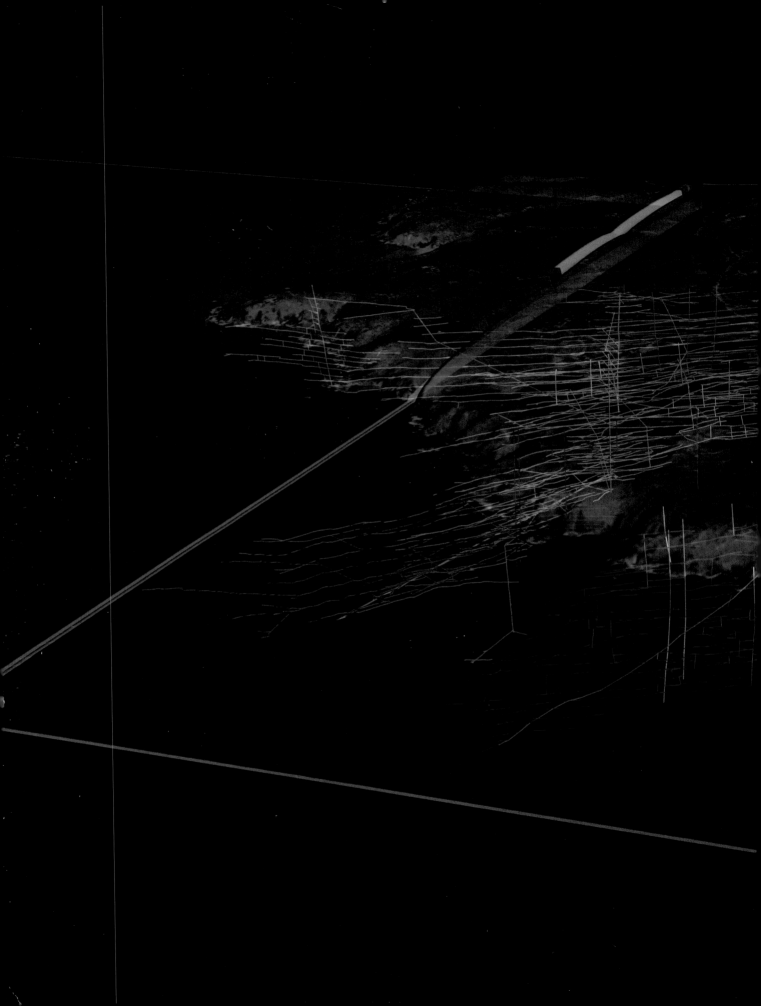

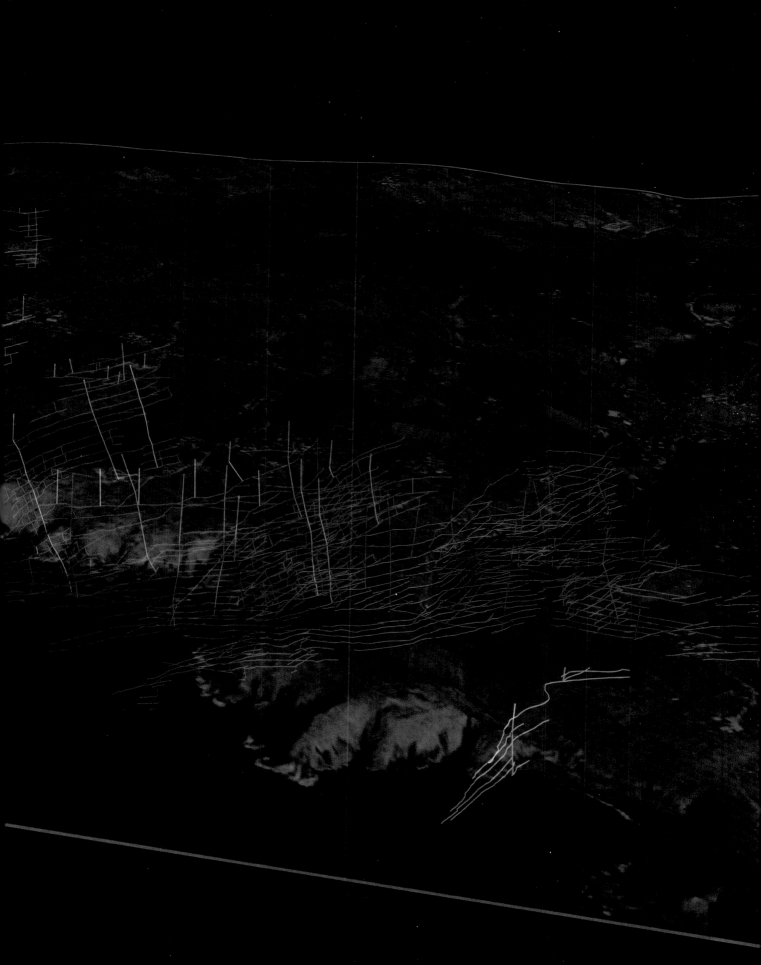

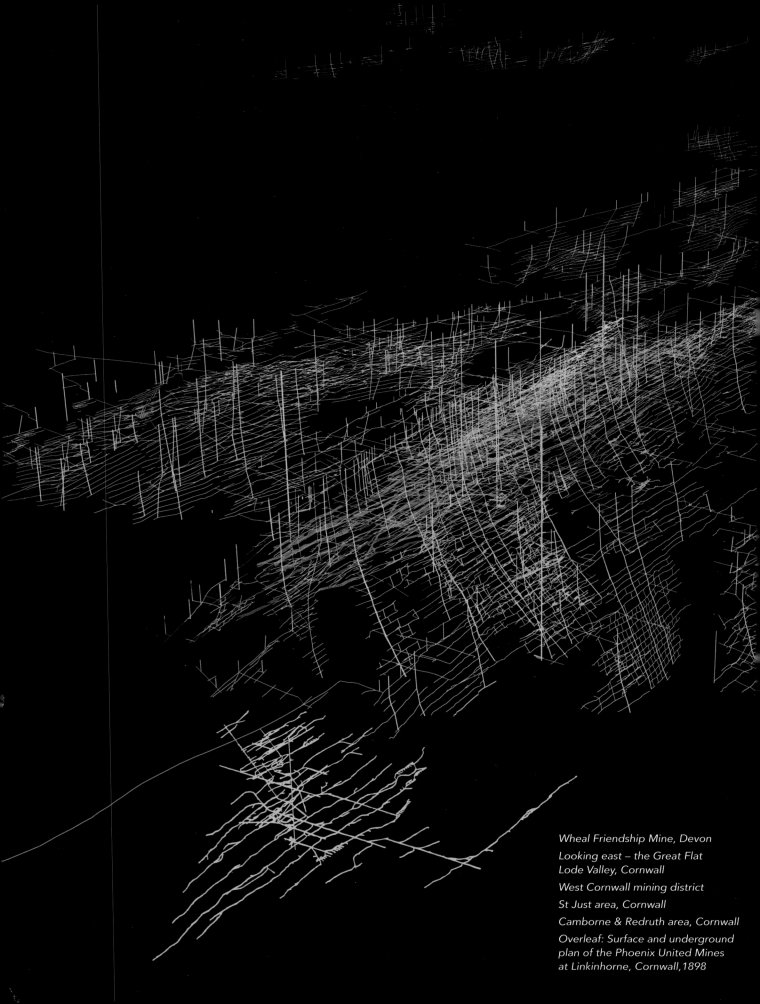

Wheal Friendship Mine, Devon

Looking east – the Great Flat
Lode Valley, Cornwall

West Cornwall mining district

St Just area, Cornwall

Camborne & Redruth area, Cornwall

Overleaf: Surface and underground
plan of the Phoenix United Mines
at Linkinhorne, Cornwall,1898

By its very nature mining is not sustainable – once you've taken it out, all that's left is a hole. These resources are finite, but if you can't grow it you have to mine it. These models also show where we can explore next.

I'm a member of a mine rescue team and I've done a lot of caving. I'm sometimes asked why it is we go underground. I wonder if it's the secretive nature of it. For me it's a need to explore a different dimension – it's an inbuilt curiosity. But it's a real challenge because all your senses are questioning what you're doing. Nature has formed these incredible caves and we want to know what's underneath the earth, to be the first people ever to see it just as miners are the first humans to see the rock face they work on.

Maps have progressed from quite a rudimentary form to being high-precision and extremely accurate. If you look at old mining maps, they are engineering masterpieces but they are incredibly artistic as well. The mine models I've created are based on engineering and yet I would say that, more than anything, they are artistic and they tell a human story. ☉

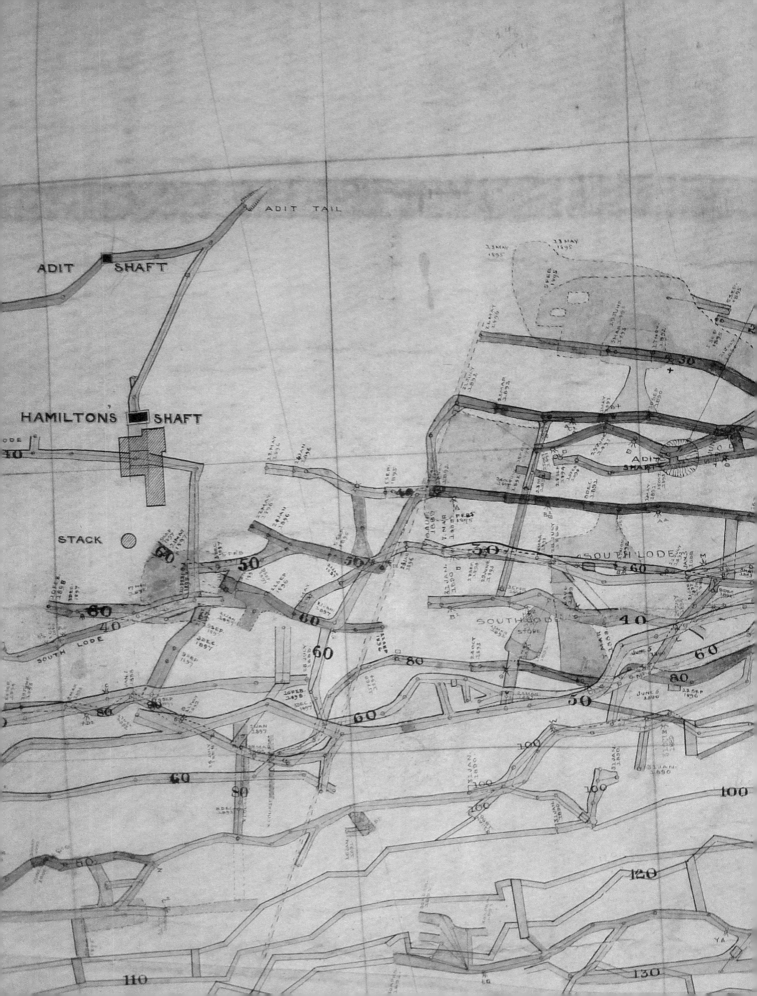

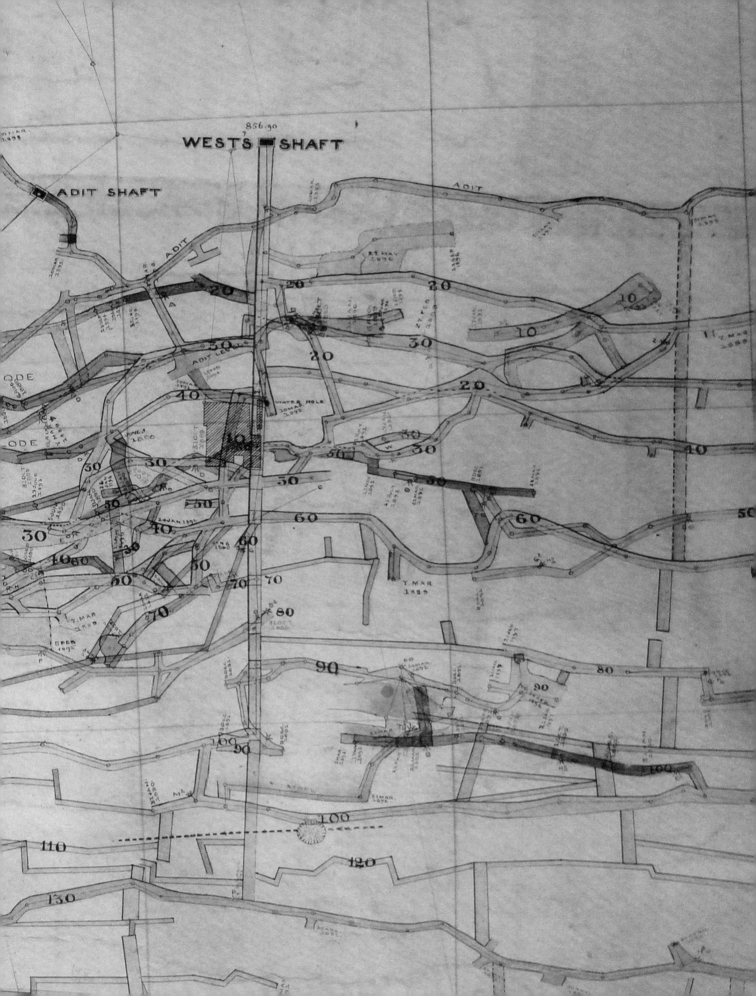

WEST'S SHAFT

ADIT SHAFT

THE BONE CAVES

HISTORY, COLOUR AND MAGIC

In the multi-coloured layers of rock that make up North West Scotland's limestone country, the dissolving power of rainwater has, over millennia, opened up crevices and widened clefts to hollow out secret honeycombs of space. Hidden within these caves we find a thousand shards of animal bones – red deer, brown bear, lynx, arctic fox, polar bear – and deeper still, cloistered human remains.

Crofter and professor of environmental change, Annie Worsley, reflects on the formation of these caves and the secrets they shelter, while poet, Kathleen Jamie, sits at the mouth of the caves where the bones of bears have slept for almost fifty thousand years.

SECRETS OF LIMESTONE AND WATER

THE CAVES OF INCHNADAMPH

Words: Annie Worsley
Illustration: Jackie Morris

In remote North West Scotland, where rock is ancient beyond imagining, sits a curl of much younger limestone. Westwards lie the oldest, hardest rocks on earth. Aquamarine Lewisian Gneiss, stippled and striped with convoluted bands of white, red and charcoal grey, were birthed in the fiery heart of ancient earth. A billion or more years later desert sands blew across the Archaean landscape, eventually settling and solidifying to form rust-brown and pink Torridonian sandstones. Much more recently ice has also played its part. For two million years the Quaternary ice sheets waxed and waned. Some wanings were subtropical, warmer even than our own Anthropocene. During the waxings mile-high ice scraped and scoured, creating the enigmatic gneiss 'cnoc and lochan' landscapes and the fantastical sandstone ramparts of monolithic mountains such as Suilven and Stac Pollaidh. Face west and the land speaks of tumult, of fire and ice. Look east and younger upstart rocks of the Moine Thrust are piled in ripples and waves of height, testament to the slow, enduring grind of tectonic force.

But this narrow stretch of limestone country, surrounded as it is by hard lands and great age, gently tells of warmer times and life-filled seas. This is now a place of softer things – scented grasses, rich soils and countless springs of sweet, clear water. Summer lingers here even as the autumn gales scurry in; the sward is not rusting but verdant and pricked with tiny stars of late-flowering herbs. And, just as with many other limestone regions in Britain, it is redolent with the stories of people. There are prehistoric chambered cairns, the rubble of houses and walls, old field systems and a Clan MacLeod castle, built more than six hundred years ago.

The ancients were drawn inexorably to limestone territory. About twelve thousand years ago, in the days of the great Wild Woods of the early Holocene, this place would have been easier to clear; its rich soils better for cultivation and grazing animals. For several thousand years people have built their homes and sheltered here. Even now, deer and sheep prefer to sip limestone spring water and nibble its tender herbs and grasses. But limestone possesses one very special secret – hidden within its layered bulk are honeycombs of space where air and water may pass unseen. It is porous and permeable. Limestone claims rainwater as its own and allows passage down cracks and fissures and through its very structure and substance. Inevitably the water moves and gathers together, dissolving rock and creating larger hollows and passageways where minerals seep and accumulate. Finally, finding a way to the outer world again, water appears in springs and sumps and the ephemeral streams that rise and fall according to limestone's whim and rainfall's fancy. This is how caves are formed – acidic water dissolving limestone at its weakest points, slowly widening clefts and opening crevices, and seeking new routes downwards, pulled always by gravity.

Streams issue from everywhere here. In one special place a valley winds eastwards, overlooked by the ramparts of aptly named Beinn an Fhuarain, 'Mountain of Springs'. I am following a path here that winds inwards beside a river and leads into the limestone itself. After the grand vistas of wild summits and open coasts the vale becomes a gorge and feels cloistered. Waterfalls sing noisily. There have been a lot of downpours recently. Usually most rain is absorbed by the ground or seeps down through the valley floor but now everywhere drips and fizzles. Water is emerging magically from within the stones and upwelling through the green turf.

As I walk up the valley I see the dark crags of the Bone Caves ahead. The rock layers are the colour of Japanese tamahagane steel used in Samurai swords, blended layers of platinum, ash and gunmetal. It is said that sword-smiths know the casting temperature of steel by its colour, and can identify the number of times the metal was forged, welded and folded from its hue and chroma. Geologists can do the same with rock strata. This limestone is testament to the warmth and abundant life of ancient seas, its tri-colour greys tell of subtle differences in formation, morphology and chemistry.

And yet I am puzzled as I clamber up the steep path and approach the caves. What seemed charcoal blue from below is now a multi-coloured micro-universe. Enormous droplets of water splash down. I pull up my hood to stop them trickling down my back. Everywhere the rocks drip and seep with liquid. Everywhere is covered by a thin, near-microscopic sheen of colour – lichens and mosses in stripes and bands

of blue and orange, vivid green and purple, pink and white. The caves themselves are in a line, their mouths varied in size and shape but all unyielding to the light. The slightly tilted rock is laminated as if sheets of limestone have been placed one on top of the other. Each cave is fronted by a welcome mat of lime green and yellow grass, mown down to fine velvet by sheep and deer, through which narrow trails disappear inside into the darkness.

Now I am sitting at the mouth of the largest cave. It is mid-October and autumn is gilding the hills with gold and copper. Even before the remnants of hurricane Ophelia have arrived in the Highlands the day is fiercely windy. Behind me the cave echoes with voices. I can hear the blind water singing deep inside the cavern. There are no other visitors to the Bone Caves but I am sure I hear the ghosts of people long gone. On the steep slopes across the valley, cloud-shadows race upwards chased hard by gusting winds. They carry the urgent roars of stags and I wonder if it is their echoing bellows I'm hearing.

Many bones have been found inside these caves. In the fine debris were a thousand shards of red deer antlers, and other caves held lynx, arctic fox, brown bear and wolf remains. I look at my dog as he stares out of the cave mouth watching the deer run below him and wonder if his wolf genes are thrumming. Deeper inside this cavern, which is quickly becoming our shelter as the winds strengthen and rain arrives in vertical silver squalls, were once human bones. Hidden in a rock niche with them was a pin made from a walrus tusk. Such a personal gift for someone once loved, a fragment of other lives hidden for millennia. And, much deeper under the mountain of springs, lies a polar bear skull. Were these remnants placed, washed in by meltwaters, trapped by hunters, or did the living go there to die? There are more questions than artefacts, more speculations than answers. Debate wafts back and forth about how the bones came to be there. But sheltering here out of the wind and rain, one reason sits at the front of my mind.

Some years ago in a summer of heat, we were caught by an unexpected thunderstorm at the summit of Stac Pollaidh, a few miles distant. Intense heat and calm were replaced in seconds by ice-cold wind and hailstones the size of peanuts. Even the deer were surprised; they flung their tawny-brown bodies against the fox-red and ginger rocks. As we struggled to put on our waterproof clothing in the buffeting gusts, lightning began to strike all around us. The flashes of fierce light were reflected in the deer's eyes; patches of thin mountain vegetation were scorched. Deafened, we scrambled down. The lightning kept striking all about us; steam hissed up in tall plumes. So we hid; in a tiny cave, under a great slab of sandstone, along with ten thousand humming bees. The roof and walls of our hideaway rippled with wings. Eventually the storm passed. The thick bee-lining began to shred; slowly, then quickly, the insects streamed out into the clearing air and spread across the purple flowering heather.

Who would not seek sanctuary from such violence in places if they could? The Bone Caves of Inchnadamph would also have provided shelter for animals and humans in times of ice and heat, and when thunderstorms strode the peaks around them.

Our afternoon begins to slip away and we ready ourselves to leave. The weather has worsened and we put on our modern waterproof clothing as hunter-gatherers would have worn deer skin. I imagine myself dressed with ornamental antlers and then laugh at the thought. In these gusts they would be torn from my head. The path down is steep and slippery in the pouring rain. It loops around the head of the valley and on the opposite side of the boulder-strewn river bed. Although the rocks are slick and wet, the river waters here are running underground.

We look back up at the crags and they are dark and drab once more. I am blown over a few times by powerful gusts, my feet uncertain, and I wish I was back in the security of the caves. All around me the limestone reflects the worsening storm in myriad greys, but I know of its secret forms; the colours and whispering magic, and its storytelling bones. ✸

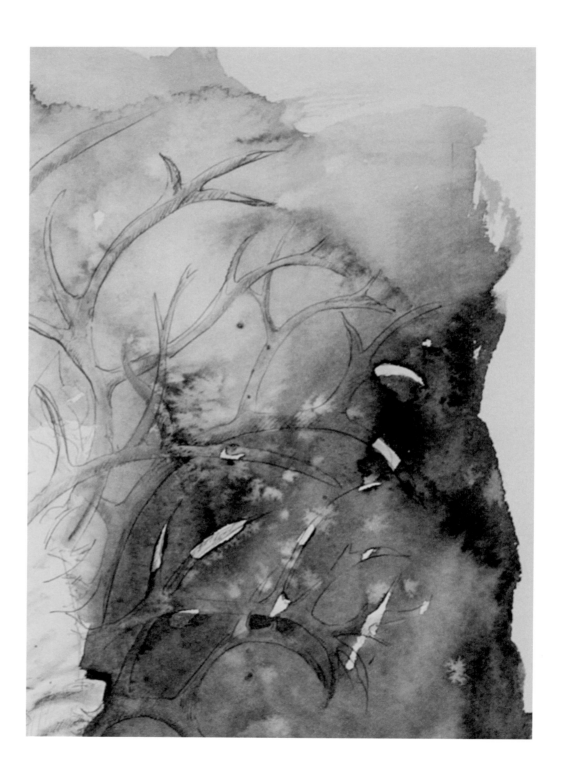

THE REINDEER CAVE

DREAM OF THE BEAR

Words: Kathleen Jamie
Illustration: Jackie Morris

You're sheltering in a cave, thinking about the Ice Age.

From the cave mouth: a West Highland landscape in early spring, sometime in
the Holocene. Maybe the late Holocene. The Anthropocene.
On the hillside opposite, six red deer have bedded down in the heather.
It's raining, a soft Highland rain, a smirr.

Not half an hour ago, you were walking beside the burn in a narrow ravine
further up the glen. You heard something, glanced up to see a large rock bounce then
plummet into the burn twenty five yards in front of you.
The echo faded but your heart was still hammering as you backed away.

They call these caves the 'Bone Caves' because of all the animal bones found
buried inside; animals long extinct in this country. You're in 'Reindeer Cave', where
antlers rather than bones were discovered. An excavation in the 1920s produced
hundreds of reindeer antlers, almost all from females.
You sit at the cave mouth, looking out at the rain, thinking about the Ice Age.
We can wait, say the hills. Take your time. You realise you haven't a clue.

The ice came and went, is that right? Ice covered land and froze the sea for
thousands of years, but now and again, every hundred thousand years or so, came milder
spells when the ice retreated, tundra formed on the land and reindeer wandered in.
Glaciers in the glens, or what became the glens.
To reach the caves, you climb a grassy slope 150 feet above the river.
You try to imagine stepping from the cave mouth onto ice and moraine.

Some years ago, cave-divers entered into this same hill by an entrance higher on the moor, by the back door, so to speak, intending to explore a system below the Bone Caves.

It makes you quail, the thought of crawling through darkness and passageways and underground streams. Echoes and falling rocks.

Deep within, the cavers found the bones of bears. What was that like? Like reaching the memory of the hill itself.

Eventually, carefully, the bones were brought to the surface. In time they were carbon dated. The oldest were 48,000 years old. A long sleep, even for a bear: sixteen million days and nights had passed in the upper world. Long enough for the ice to return, then yield again, then return in one last snap, then leave for good – or at least for now.

The cave mouth the bear must have used has since been blocked by the rocky detritus of that last ice-grip, the one which ended 10,000 years ago and bequeathed us the land we know.

10,000 years – in the great scheme of things, we're living through a warm bank-holiday weekend.

As to the antlers, they were found before carbon dating became available. Then, excited speculation concerned us – people, humans! Might there have been Paleolithic humans here, to gather up all those antlers and store them in a cave? But there's no evidence for that. Female reindeer, caribou, shed their antlers naturally, up on the calving grounds, and some antlers must have fallen onto the glacier to be borne downhill and swilled into the cave mouth by meltwater, and duly buried. That's the surmise.

The hoard of antlers is kept in the store of the National Museum of Scotland. They're not as you might imagine, not majestic. Ancient fragments, they look more like broken biscuits. Also in the store, wrapped in a box, are the bear bones including a brown-stained skull. The skull was in the cave and what was in the skull? Bear mind, bear memory – when autumn came and the nights began to freeze, he remembered where the cave was, as he padded across the glacier.

Also stored away are the remains of other creatures of the caves; lynx, for example. Even the tiny bones of lemmings, saved for the nation in an old Cadbury's chocolate tin.

The world warms. Last winter was the wettest; no snow or ice to speak of, a flash of blue sky was rare as a comet, the nights were starless and lachrymose. The TV news showed floods and sandbags, householders weeping as they cleared the sodden mess. There were arguments about land management, flood plains, deforestation. Commentators intoned, 'is it climate change?'
Well, you thought sourly, if it walks like a duck and quacks like a duck, it's a duck.

Where do we come from? What are we? Where are we going? At your cave mouth, you wonder if the ice will ever return, a natural cycle, or if we've gone too far with our Anthropocene. But who can answer that? We just can't grasp the scale of our species' effects, but the single falling stone that could smash our brains out – that we understand.

Now the rain's easing, and a scruffy brown terrier appears at the cave mouth. Following the dog come children. Their voices carry from down the slope: Daddy! Look! The caves!

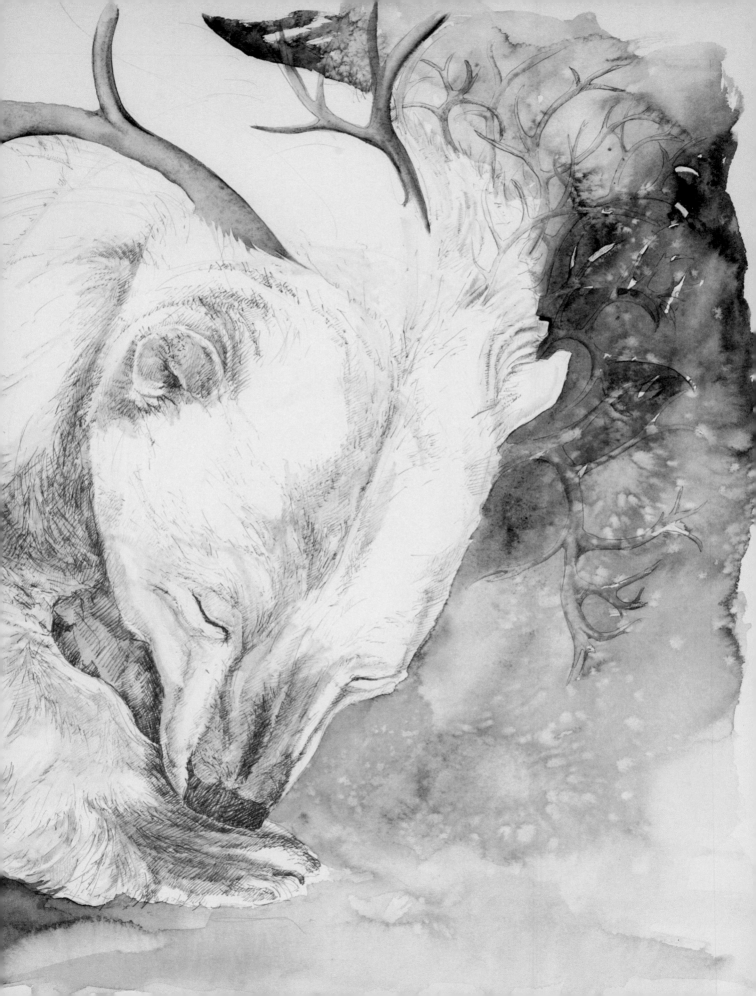

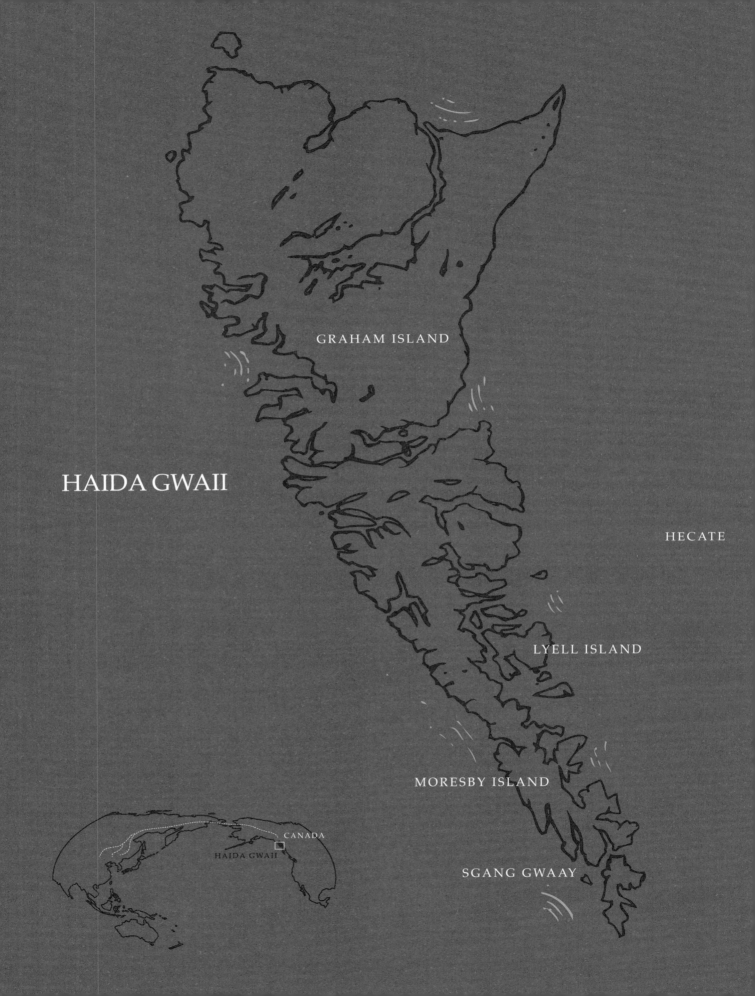

HAIDA GWAII

GRAHAM ISLAND

HECATE

LYELL ISLAND

MORESBY ISLAND

SGANG GWAAY

CANADA

HAIDA GWAII

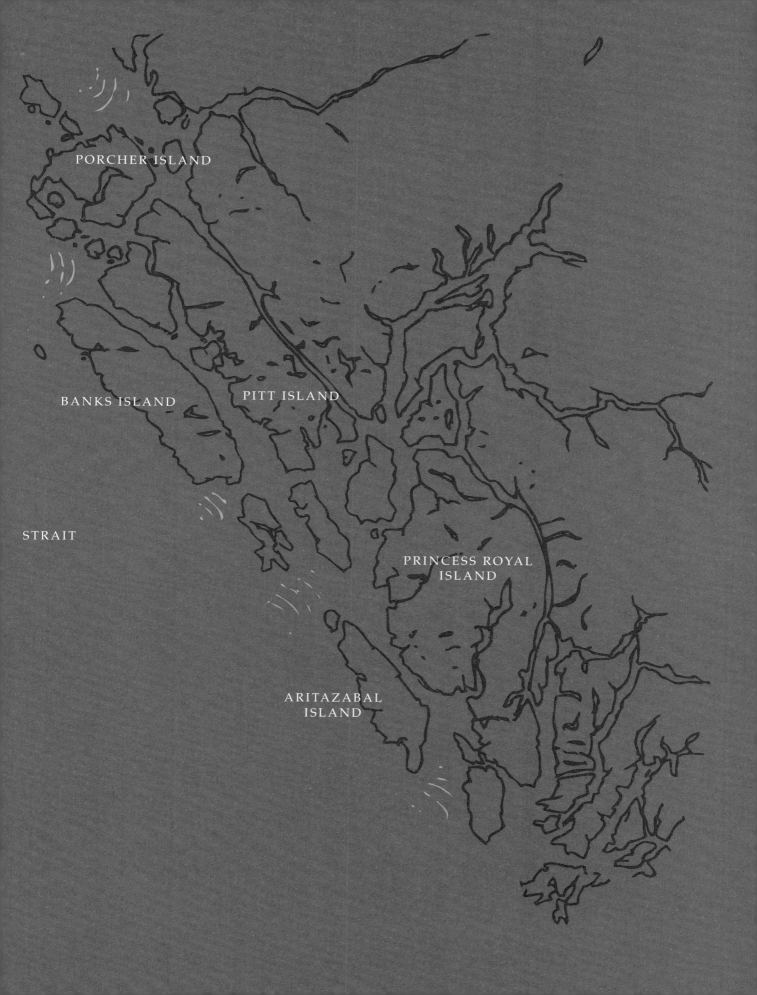

PORCHER ISLAND

BANKS ISLAND

PITT ISLAND

STRAIT

PRINCESS ROYAL
ISLAND

ARITAZABAL
ISLAND

HAIDA GWAII

ISLANDS OF THE PEOPLE

Photography: Owen Perry

Haida Gwaii is an archipelago on the north coast of British Columbia, Canada, consisting of two main islands – Graham Island to the north, Moresby Island to the south – and around 150 smaller islands, a combined landmass of just under 4,000 square miles. Hecate Strait separates it from the mainland to the east; to the west is the Pacific Ocean. Xaadala Gwayee, an older version of the name, translates as 'islands at the boundary of the world', an apt description of its location.

Sitting at the boundary with Asia, these islands were one of the first places to be peopled in the New World as the ice sheet began to melt some 16,000 years ago. It is home to some of the earliest Paleo-Indian archaeological sites and one of the oldest traceable populations in the Americas. In 1787, George Dixon, captain of the ship the *Queen Charlotte*, named the islands after his vessel, itself named after the wife of King George III, and it was not until 2010 that the name Haida Gwaii – 'islands of the people' – was formally adopted to honour the history and culture of the Haida.

The climate is mild and wet with frequent daily rainfall; the islands themselves heavily forested and home to a variety of large trees such as red alder, yellow cedar, and shore pine. The abundant fauna includes the largest subspecies of black bear, *Ursus americanus carlottae*.

This is a dynamic region. The islands are located on a significant fault line and there are regular earthquakes as well as a history of volcanic activity. Tow Hill, on the north end of the Naikoon Peninsula on Graham Island, is a volcanic plug formed of faceted basalt columns that cooled about two million years ago. The islands themselves sit on the edge of the continental shelf that slopes sharply into the Pacific. Marine life is abundant in the sparkling waters.

Of all the peoples of the northwest coast, the Haida were renowned as carvers and painters, their work taking the form of totem poles, long-house front poles and mortuary columns carved from the giant cedars. These were typically painted black, red and green, the zoomorphic figures representing bears and killer whales, ravens and eagles that tell the stories of a clan's matrilineal lines and mythologies. Among them, the raven and the eagle are most prominent – each Haida child is given an allegiance at birth, Raven or Eagle according to the mother's heritage, which determines their life path. Raven must marry Eagle.

The most extensive and culturally significant collection of carving is found on SGang Gwaay, which translates as 'red cod island', a tiny landmass in the most southerly part of the archipelago, now a UNESCO World Heritage Site. Here the carved mortuary and memorial poles are at their most iconic and atmospheric, left standing in their original rainforest landscape in a village unoccupied since 1880 and protected by site guardians known as Watchmen.

From the late eighteenth century European travellers and traders brought conflict and illness to these islands as well as demand for fur and gold. Skirmishes with the Haida were common, often resulting in the loss of ships and lives. The discovery of gold on Moresby Island led to a gold rush in the early 1850s that fuelled the hostility, and by the late 1800s war and disease had reduced the Haida population from around 8,000 to under 600.

Throughout the twentieth century exploitation of the rich natural resources continued, with corporate logging companies decimating the ancient forests. But in 1985 the Haida Nation engaged in direct action, blocking logging roads on Lyell Island and, through the subsequent media coverage, raising awareness of the unbridled destruction. Within a few years, much of the south of the islands had gained National Park status and legal protection, and Haida villages and culture are thriving, with new prospects emerging from a focus on traditional arts and crafts and woodworking. ✸

A journal of nature & story